smotherley

Snilesworth Moor

Kepwick

Whitby

Old Byland

Cold Kirby

Helmsley

Husthwaite

ourn

Nether Poppleton

Wetherby
Leeds

THE DIARY
of a
YORKSHIRE
VET

JULIAN NORTON

GREAT-N-ORTHERN

Great Northern Books Limited
PO Box 1380, Bradford, BD5 5FB
www.greatnorthernbooks.co.uk

ISBN: 978-1-912101-80-1

Design and layout: David Burrill

CIP Data
A catalogue for this book is available from the British Library

For my friends in Thirsk

Introduction

It's been another interesting year for my family and for me, and a challenging one. While the filming of *The Yorkshire Vet* has continued, with all that it entails, I have also had the huge upheaval of having to change jobs. For many people, changing jobs is probably not such a trauma, but for me, it certainly was. I have been based at Skeldale Veterinary Centre in Thirsk, for most of the last twenty-one years. It has been more than just a job; it has been a vocation, part of my life and at times, most of my life, forging my identity as a person as well as a vet.

At the beginning of 2017, I can honestly say that I could not have envisaged my career being in any better place. Life was busy but good. Work was busy but good. Clients were happy and clients were friends. Thirsk, where my family and I had made our home, was bustling and buoyant. Yet, as the year progressed, the change that I had never thought would occur became increasingly inevitable and unavoidable, despite my utmost efforts. By the end of the year, I had left the practice that I loved, to make a new veterinary life for myself elsewhere. I do not want to dwell on the details, but the slowly dawning inevitability of the end of an era – not just for me, but for the most historic practice in the country, and arguably the world – runs as a backdrop to the stories in this short book.

I thoroughly enjoyed writing my previous two books – *Horses, Heifers and Hairy Pigs – The Life of a Yorkshire Vet* and *A Yorkshire Vet Through the Seasons*, in which I recollected past stories, experiences and pleasures from my veterinary life, and my weekly column in the *Yorkshire Post* has been scratching my new-found literary itch. The column allows me to look back over my week's patients, recall the details of interesting cases and interesting owners, and to put some thought into all the aspects of each case. It feels a little bit like writing a diary of my work. Out and about on farms, at talks and book events, or even at the surgery, it surprises me just how many people make comment upon the things I have written in my few paragraphs in the "Country Week" each Saturday.

"What *was* wrong with that chap's cows, in the end? *Did* they have iodine deficiency?" or

"I loved your story about my dog and I couldn't stop laughing. But, honestly, there was no need to change his name!"

and, quite often,

"I'm very pleased to meet you Julian. I watch your programme on channel 5, but I *love* reading your column on Saturdays." Or, conversely,

"I don't really watch much television, but I do read the paper and I always like to read your piece in the *Yorkshire Post*".

In a way, I am carrying on the family tradition. My father used to write for the same newspaper, as an athletics and sports correspondent (in fact, he still does, although not as much). I remember how, when I was a young boy, he would spend an hour or so on a Sunday evening, dictating – down the telephone – his weekly round-up of results from Cleckheaton track or the various road, cross country or fell races around the county. It is so much easier these days. My column can be emailed in, at any time of the week, day or night, along with a high definition photo of a patient or place.

So, as the autumn passed, the idea of creating a diary-style book, based around the weekly stories from the *Yorkshire Post*, seemed feasible and appealing. I contacted my editor Ben Barnett at the *Yorkshire Post* to see what he thought of the idea. Within a week, I was in discussions with a Yorkshire publisher – and this book is the result.

I hope you will enjoy it. It is a briefer book than my others and it is not intended to be a serious read, but something into which you can dip in and out; read a couple of stories in the bath or before bed, and in any order you fancy; or give as a Christmas present to your Gran.

TB Testing and Molly with a Head Injury

3rd January

Poor old Molly had got herself into trouble. The elderly terrier had started to fight with another dog, whilst out on her walk. The fracas was getting serious and no one dared put out a hand to separate the scrapping dogs, for fear of being bitten. Eventually, one of the owners intervened with his boot. Completely by accident, Molly felt the full force of the boot, reeled on the floor and promptly passed out.

There was a panic-stricken phone call to the surgery and a message appeared on the computer, saying *"Dog on way – unconscious"*. It sounded serious and it was serious. When she arrived, Molly had regained consciousness but she was still very dazed. She couldn't stand and couldn't coordinate her legs. Her front left leg seemed to be paralysed, and was buckling under her, while her back right leg was rigid. I examined her neurological system, using a tendon hammer to assess her reflexes and an ophthalmoscope to look at the optic disks at the back of her eyes. Sure enough, Molly had "papilloedema", or swelling of the optic disc – a sign of brain swelling caused by the head trauma.

I immediately admitted her for urgent treatment to reduce this swelling. She would be spending several days in the practice, under the supervision of our fantastic nurses. Time would tell whether she would make a full or a partial recovery. Just as is the case with human patients who have suffered a head injury, it is difficult to prognosticate how a case will progress.

Meanwhile, I had other jobs to keep me busy. A group of cattle, purchased from Derbyshire, needed a "post-movement TB test".

Opposite: Molly was left very shaken, suffering
from severe concussion after her accident.
We all hoped she would pull through.

The cattle had come from a suckler herd close to an active area of TB. Post-movement tests are a way of trying to stop the spread of this historic disease, although despite the best efforts of DEFRA, bovine TB does not seem to be getting any closer to coming under control. As I clipped off hair from the right side of the neck of each of these young cattle, measured the skin thickness with callipers in the semi-dark cattle shed and injected the two doses of tuberculin, I reflected that I was carrying out exactly the same procedure that had been performed before me by generations of veterinary surgeons over more than 60 years. So much for advances in veterinary science! Accurate as the test is supposed to be, there must surely be a more modern way. Nevertheless, this is how we do it. We inject the intradermal tuberculin and measure the skin lumps three days later (with that same set of brass callipers used by the practice for the last sixty years). Everyone crossed their fingers for a Friday free of skin lumps.

Scott, Molly's owner, had been crossing his fingers for days too. She showed marginal improvements as the days passed, but progress was painfully slow. She could still not control her front left leg and, more worryingly, she had not passed any urine or faeces. Had the damage to her brain resulted in a permanent paralysis of her bladder? I could not tell. So, you can imagine my excitement when I saw a small pile of poo in Molly's kennel at my 2am check. Molly's bowels were working! By the following morning, she was urinating and there was no more need to catheterise her bladder. By the end of the week she could stand unaided and walk, although with something of a curved path. She could go home with an upbeat prognosis – she was as happy as everyone to be getting back to her family.

Happy days – the TB test was clear too!

Leptospirosis

10th January

If you type "Leptospirosis" into any search engine, and read through the risk factors for contracting this nasty bacterial infection, you can see why I might be more aware of the disease than most. Participants in open water swimming (tick), rowers (tick) and veterinary surgeons (tick again) are all near the top of the list of those at risk.

Leptospirosis is not just common in these circles, though. Cows and dogs can also be affected. In cattle, the disease causes reduced fertility and, in pregnant animals, abortion. When a dog succumbs, however, the consequences are life threatening. The strain of "Lepto" that we most commonly see in dogs causes sudden onset liver and kidney failure. An unvaccinated dog which plays near a river or drinks dirty water from ditches, or one that spends time catching rats is particularly at risk. While there is no vaccine to protect against leptospirosis in humans, both cattle and dogs can be vaccinated routinely, which makes it all the more frustrating when we see a case.

With two vets in the house, mealtime conversations at home often revolve around interesting cases, difficult diagnoses or challenging clients. As I dished out the risotto, Anne told me about a young spaniel she was treating. Her boss had described the jaundiced spaniel as "more yellow than Bananaman's wallet". Its liver and kidney parameters were off the scale and it was desperately poorly. The dog's vaccines had lapsed, and it lived on a farm near the river. The finger of suspicion pointed towards infection with Leptospira.

Sadly, two days later, despite intensive treatment, the spaniel died. The owner's funds did not stretch as far as post-mortem and lab tests. It can be expensive to get a definitive diagnosis, requiring a test called a Polymerase Chain Reaction to identify the bacteria, and it was more important to get all his other dogs up to date with their vaccines.

So, when I heard that Benson, a four-year-old Labrador, had been rushed to the practice, collapsed and yellow, my suspicions were raised. He had been treated at another practice, but his owner (whose daughter was at school with one of my sons) had decided that I was the person to treat the dog. Unfortunately, I was already out on my rounds, blood-testing bulls when they arrived, so Benson saw a colleague. Benson was showing signs of multiple organ failure, with dramatic jaundice. The whites of his eyes, his gums and his skin were all also "as yellow as Bananaman's wallet". Despite aggressive treatment, Benson deteriorated rapidly, and he did not make it to the end of the day.

I called his owner to explain the situation, and discuss the possibility of Lepto. I enquired about his vaccination status and asked whether he ever walked near a river or a lake.

"Oh, yes. He's always in the river," she confirmed. "We walk him there every day. He's always drinking dirty water from the river. I wish he wouldn't, but it's not easy to stop him. He's a typical Labrador. Well, he was a typical Labrador." She broke down in tears.

Benson had lived within a few miles of the spaniel Anne had been treating, and it seemed eminently plausible that both young, water-loving dogs had succumbed to the same, fatal disease. I talked through the intricacies of diagnosis and the need for post-mortem samples to make a definitive diagnosis. Clearly further testing would not help Benson, or his family (the other pet they owned was a cat, mercifully not at risk). It was a stark and tragic reminder that the diseases against which we vaccinate are horrible ones – that's why we do it.

Lost Cat and the Swan with a Pouch

17th January

Thursday had its ups and downs. My first patient was an odd one. It was Bella the black swan. She came in with her partner, Buster and their owner, Kirsty. Kirsty and her two swans, both wrapped in cloths fastened securely with masking tape (to avoid damage to their wings on the journey), made an unusual sight in the waiting room.

The graceful bird had been struggling with a recurrent swelling under her beak. Food was getting impacted under Bella's tongue, making it difficult for her to eat. Kirsty was having to keep the swans in a shed, away from grass, to prevent it from getting worse. She told me that she had been doing some research and that, "in the olden days, people would put a pebble in and sew up the hole." This sounded an unsuitable thing to do in modern veterinary practice, but it gave me a clue about what the problem might be. The description of placing a pebble and then sewing over the top, suggested that there must be some kind of acquired pouch under the tongue that was filling up with food. I had no intention of placing any pebbles inside it, but if I could safely place the swan under anaesthetic and identify the edges, I felt sure I could suture the pouch closed.

I examined Bella as best I could and, sure enough, there was a pocket of impacted food under her tongue, about as big as a marble. The anaesthetic went smoothly and, with Bella lying still, it was much easier to see what was going on. Under the base of her tongue was, as expected, a pouch of baggy membrane, now free of food, but sure to fill up again shortly. I managed to place sutures and close off the orifice, just like stitching across the pocket of a pair of trousers. In the same way that the trouser pocket wouldn't take a set of car keys once it was sewn up, now Bella wouldn't keep getting grass building up under her tongue.

I felt happy that we'd achieved some success with this unusual condition, but only time would tell.

The nurses and I hoped we would have the same success in reuniting an elderly, lost cat with her owners. The geriatric cat was brought in to us after she was found wandering around in someone's garden. She didn't have a microchip and, as is often the case, the help of the local vet had been sought. "Do you recognise this cat?"

But nobody recognised her and "Gwenny" had been with us for several days. It looked as if she would be finding a home with one of our staff. But the "share" button of our Facebook page had disseminated the story of Gwenny as far as Nether Poppleton. A family who had lost their cat six months previously ("we think it climbed into a removal van") had seen Gwenny and sent photos to us by email. A collection of optimistic vets, nurses and camera crew were all convinced that the tabby cat in our kennels and the tabby cat from Nether Poppleton were one and the same.

We all waited with excitement for the emotional reunion. Gwenny stalked along the top of the reception desk, head held high, but without a glimmer of recognition. The husband, wife and five-year old-son were silent. They shook their heads in unison. "That's not our cat."

Much as we all tried to persuade them that she *must* be their cat (I tried to convince them that six months of sleeping in a bush would surely mute the colours somewhat), it clearly wasn't a match.

"If you can't find her owners by next week, let us know and we'll have her," they said as they left. No need, though. Gwenny has a queue of potential new owners, slugging it out to give the lovely old cat a home!

Opposite: Bella and her friend, wrapped in sheets, awaiting my examination. As ever, interesting cases are pursued by a camera.

Early Morning Calf Bed

24th January

Being on second call is a strange thing. The vet on first call is taking responsibility for everything that comes in, so it is generally quiet, but when the second on call vet is needed, it is usually urgent. Emma, the vet on first, needed some assistance early this morning. I set off straight away. It was still dark and gloomy when I got to the farm. The thick fog stubbornly refused to lift from the fields and lanes along the river Ure. The problem was plain to see though. The poor cow, having given birth to twins in the early hours, now had her whole, very large uterus hanging out, covered in mud and the remains of the afterbirth. It was the size of a sack of potatoes. Emma knew she would need a hand to get it back in.

Replacing a uterine prolapse in a cow is physically challenging and requires the correct technique and, ideally, some experience. It is also a very dirty job. One famous veterinary surgeon – a friend of Alf Wight – apparently advocated the removal of *all of the vet's clothes* before attempting this procedure, to avoid soiling them with blood and mud and other goo and debris. It was a bit cold for that this morning.

Once we had restrained the cow, we gave her an epidural. This would numb the area, providing pain relief and it would also stop her from straining – a natural reflex, but one that was not at all helpful at this stage. We would never be able to replace this 30kg sack of potatoes, slimy and delicate, without everything being relaxed. The epidural worked a treat. When her tail went flaccid,

Opposite: A "calf bed" otherwise known as a prolapsed uterus is a serious and messy problem. This case, early one morning, was a tough start to a winter's day.

we knew we were in business. She was still standing up, which offered some advantages – we had gravity on our side. Once the large viscus was fed back into the vulva, it should slide back down into the abdomen. If a cow is down, unable to stand through weakness or fatigue, she needs to be positioned in a very specific way to facilitate the procedure, which is reasonably tricky.

We both worked carefully and painstakingly to persuade the organ back into its proper place, sweat dripping from our foreheads. As predicted, blood and gloopy fluids were everywhere – inside and outside of waterproof clothing. It was one of the toughest prolapses I had done in twenty-one years of practise and I sympathised with Emma, it being one of her first. Finally, the bloody, slimy sack of potatoes was back inside the cow.

"Well done! Good job! Thank goodness for that!" exclaimed the farmers, although I did not share their relief just yet. Sadly, the success was temporary. The cow gave a large groan and spewed her uterus straight back out. Then she promptly collapsed onto the ground. Another twenty minutes and more groaning – this time from the vets and not the cow – and the pesky thing was back in, inverted and all was good.

Next, we needed to place some large and strong sutures across the vulva to stop the uterus from prolapsing again. Once she had been given some antibiotics to reduce the possibility of sepsis and some more painkillers the patient was suddenly looking 100% better. Her chances of survival had improved dramatically. After some serious action with the hosepipe and a scrubbing brush, I was ready to return to the surgery – I had a dog, Rufus, whose eye I needed to recheck and I didn't want to be late.

Rufus was, thankfully, much better, but despite my successful treatment of his sore eye, his owner viewed me with suspicion. It was only later that I realised I still had a large smear of blood across my forehead that the hosepipe had not quite reached!

Early Morning. Again.

31st January

Nights on call have been busy over the last few weeks. Ewes are lambing and cows are calving and, at least when I'm on duty, they always seem to get into difficulty during the small hours.

1.35 in the morning is a bad time for a phone call. I was fast asleep when the phone rang and the last thing I wanted to hear was, "I've got a cow calving. The feet are big and I think she needs a caesarean."

I assured John, the farmer, that I'd be with him as soon as I could. As I rummaged about for my clothes in the darkness, I did some quick calculations: five minutes to get dressed, two minutes to call the camera crew, twenty-five minutes to the farm. If it was a quick calving it might take twenty minutes, maybe thirty. If John's prediction was correct and a caesarean section was needed it would be an hour if all went smoothly, but an hour and a half if not. Ten minutes to wash off and tidy up, twenty-five minutes to drive home. I'd be back in bed between half past three and half past four. That would only give me two or three hours sleep before getting up time, and I was already tired.

But I'd been here a hundred times before and I knew it would get better. Night-time calls to deliver baby animals are like getting up early to go for a run; it is *definitely* worth it once you get going. The camera crew were not at all convinced though, and anyway, John was not keen on sharing his favourite cow's delivery with the nation on television, so they got to stay tucked up in bed, while I wound my way through the dark lanes of North Yorkshire, struggling to focus on the road.

John and his son had everything ready when I arrived. Sure enough, the calf's feet were big and the cow's pelvis was narrow. Tentative pulling yielded no movement at all and we both agreed

the best solution was to "take it out the side". While I administered an epidural, injected local anaesthetic and clipped and prepped the area, John (much to my delight) produced a folding-leaf table for my surgical kit. Though I was very tired, at least my back would be saved the extra strain of bending over a kit balanced in the straw, in these early hours.

The op went very well – text book in fact – and I was washing the tenacious, congealed blood from my chest and arms within an hour, with a happy cow and a healthy calf lifting its head, sticking its tongue out and peering about in a bemused fashion. I had lost track of my earlier mental maths in the excitement of bringing a new life into the world. A glance at my phone confirmed it was just before three in the morning; not too bad, I thought.

As we watched the mother and baby get to know one another, I reflected on where I had been twenty-four hours previously. I had been weaving my way back to the hotel, in my dinner suit, following the after-show party of the National Television Awards, where I had rubbed shoulders with such great names as David Attenborough, Paul O'Grady and my namesake Graham. Though we were not nominees, a (very) small group from The Yorkshire Vet team were lucky enough to have been invited as guests. It was amazing to be there, just metres from the stage. It was a fantastic and glittering evening, which, to be fair, was the reason I was so tired tonight. It was so utterly different to my normal life. But, fabulous as it was, if I had to choose, I would take the early hours on a North Yorkshire farm with a newly calved cow and her calf any day!

Opposite: A healthy, strong, newborn calf is always a lovely sight and brings a wonderful sense of achievement, especially in the middle of the night.

Opal the Comfortable Ferret

7th February

Wednesday morning's ops list was going smoothly. The first procedure was a simple castration in a compliant cocker spaniel called Wilson. This was followed by an equally straightforward lumpectomy in a yellow Labrador. The first half of the morning had been very relaxed and altogether normal. As I briefly perused the other patients in the kennels, it looked eminently likely that there might even be time for a mid-morning coffee break.

However, the illusion of peace and tranquillity was soon to be broken by two, more unusual patients. One, safe in a carrying cage at the far end of the kennels, was resting peacefully in her fleecy hammock. She was as blissfully unaware of what awaited her, just as I had been unaware of her presence in the kennels. Opal was a four-year-old jill – a female ferret. She was due to be spayed, but was so comfortable that she was fast asleep even before her anaesthetic had been administered. Ferrets love to curl up in a hammock and Opal was no exception. I felt terribly mean having to disturb her to give her the stinging injection, but it was important for today's procedure and it was soon done. Opal rushed back into her hammock, curled up again and drifted back into unconsciousness, this time induced by the anaesthetic and so possibly with slightly more hallucinogenic dreams than she had enjoyed previously.

Spaying a ferret does not rank high on the list of common procedures for most veterinary clinics, but it is actually a fairly simple operation to perform, and today's op went well. The

Opposite: This ferret made itself comfortable in its hammock whilst she awaited her place in theatre!

process is very similar to spaying a cat or a bitch. Both ovaries and also the uterus are removed, so pregnancy is prevented and seasons no longer occur. This is especially important in ferrets because they are what are known as "induced ovulators". This means that females stay in season until they are mated, at which point ovulation takes place, and the season comes to an end. If the jill is not mated, and the season goes on for a long time, an excessive amount of oestrogen builds up in the blood stream. This can be very hazardous to the body as the high hormone levels eventually suppress the bone marrow, and this in turn leads to a severe anaemia, which can be life threatening. There are various ways to prevent this unfortunate consequence of these high levels of sex hormone. One method uses a hormone implant or injection to reduce the oestrus activity. Another solution is to acquire a vasectomised male ferret, to allow uninhibited matings to occur, inducing ovulation and thus bringing the season to an end. This works very well. The result is one happy pair of ferrets, no oestrogen-induced bone marrow suppression for the jill and no babies. However, it is an extremely fiddly procedure for the vet, and the op is fraught with potential difficulties.

For Opal, though, an unfettered sex life was not to be. She would not be troubled by hormones again, as I delved into her abdomen, identified and ligated each of her ovaries and then her cervix, and lifted out the whole reproductive tract. Neatly sutured, and pain relief administered, she was soon back in her cage and snoozing again in her hammock. As she slowly woke up, a palm tree, some lapping waves and a pina colada could hardly have made her look more relaxed. I guessed though, that she wasn't dreaming about a lifelong love affair with her favourite male ferret!

Maverick the Buzzard

14th February

I'd met Maverick the Red-Tailed Buzzard before. He had been rushed to see me by his previous owner, as a young chick. The greedy buzzard swallowed his food far too quickly and this had led to a serious condition, similar to "sour crop" in a chicken. He had deteriorated rapidly. By the time he arrived at the practice he was at death's door. None of us had given him much chance of survival. He was young, weak and floppy. Any condition which develops rapidly is more serious than a slowly progressing one, yet somehow, to everyone's surprise and delight, the treatment worked and the little buzzard rose, like Lazarus, after a day or so of intensive care.

A year later, Maverick was registered with new owners, also knowledgeable and experienced in the management of raptors, and he and I were faced with another serious ailment, albeit one that was much less acute. Maverick was suffering from a condition called "Bumblefoot". Whilst this may sound like the name of a fluffy creature who collects rubbish on Wimbledon Common, it is actually a very nasty problem affecting birds. Its technical name is pododermatitis – an inflammatory condition of the underside of the foot. Ulceration of the surface develops and dried-up pus accumulates under the skin of the bird's foot, extending around the tendons and other important structures. The pain associated with the lesions causes the bird to shift its weight unevenly, resulting in the problem spreading to adjacent areas and often to the other foot. Mild cases can be treated with some success using antibiotics for extended periods, but if the condition is advanced or severe, surgery to resect the affected tissue is often the only course of action.

I'd treated several birds like this before, but I needed to check that Sally, the theatre nurse for the week, was happy to do the

Maverick the Buzzard had a condition called "Bumblefoot".
It's more serious than its name suggests.

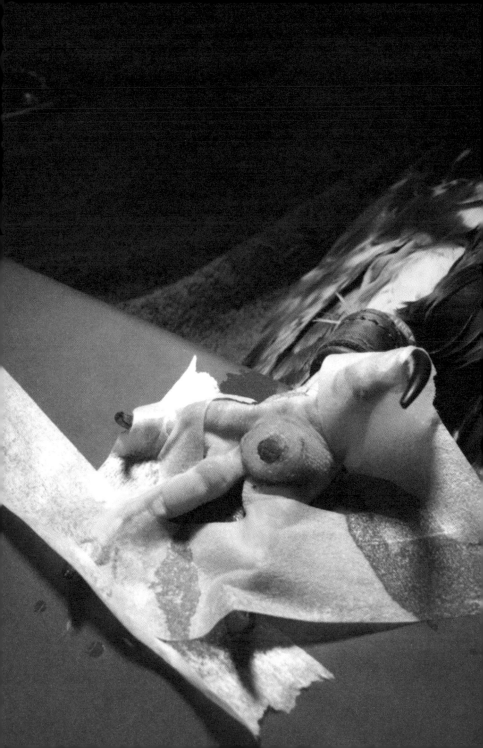

anaesthetic.

"Yes, brilliant! I like a challenge," she confirmed in her typically cheery manner.

So, Maverick arrived at the practice as planned, in a large wooden box. The bird who emerged was very different to the one I had seen before. Whilst he clearly wasn't the world's best example of a Red-Tailed Buzzard – his neonatal illness had obviously left him weak and somewhat stunted – he was now fully grown and fully fledged. I was pleased to see him again. His foot didn't look great though. It was a classic example of Bumblefoot and I knew it would be difficult to effect a complete cure, but I had saved him once and I would do my best to save him again.

Sally and I took him through to theatre, gauntlet in place and jesses around his feet. The gaseous induction worked well and he was quickly asleep. We managed to tape his talons open on a suitable padded surface to allow me surgical access. With the skin of his foot scrubbed and prepped, I could excise neatly all around the marble-sized mass of inspissated pus that was deforming a large part of his foot. I'd hoped to make a natty curved incision to put the healing wound to one side of the surgical site, but this was not possible as I dissected out the yellow, cheesy goo and removed the black, necrotic centre.

Some saline irrigation, antibiotic powder and four, absorbable simple interrupted sutures later, Maverick's left foot looked much healthier. We applied a small, cushioning dressing and Sally and I congratulated ourselves on a good job, well done.

"That went well," she said. "It's the first bird of prey I've ever anaesthetised."

I'd have never guessed.

He has Pants on his Head.

21st February

"Thank you so much. I'm sorry for bothering you. He has pants on his head now and that is much better."

This was the last in a series of emails I received on Tuesday evening, from a worried owner called Nicky.

It had been a very busy couple of days and I was nearly asleep in a comfy chair, upstairs in the practice, where we had been chatting about all the cases we had seen. I pulled myself out of the chair before sleep overcame me, and set about my inbox.

Nicky had sent a message, asking for advice.

"It's my dog Hobbo. He's cut his ear and it's bleeding. Is it best to pop him down now or leave it 'til tomorrow?"

I emailed back, asking for more details of the injury. The reply suggested it wasn't too serious, so I offered some tips on how to stem the flow of blood and stop the kitchen from being splattered. Cut ears can spread what looks like a huge amount of blood over a large area, very quickly. A pair of pants was the perfect solution. Bizarre as it seemed to be reading a message about a dog who was wearing pants on his head, I was pleased to hear that the problem was solved. I was also happy that Hobbo didn't need my veterinary attention, as it was my only night off of the week and I was keen to get home. It was my wife, Anne's, birthday so we were hoping to have an evening without dogs, cats, cows or sheep.

Sadly, even without a beeper in my pocket, this was not to be. Even before the birthday meal had been created, my mobile was ringing.

"Can yer come and lamb us a sheep?" I recognised Rodney's voice immediately. His was the furthest farm from the practice and I knew that if I went to see his sheep, I would not be back home until late.

"I'm sorry, Rodney. I'm not on call tonight and I'm supposed to be having dinner with my wife. I'll call my colleague, Candella – she's on duty and she's very good at lambing."

"Aye, all raight. Sorry to bother you," he said, and with that he was off. And within five minutes, so was Candella, heading out to West Yorkshire to lamb Rodney's sheep.

Next was a "bing" from the same pesky mobile (which I really should have switched off by this time, but hadn't). It was a text from a farmer whose goats I was visiting in the morning.

"When you come tomorrow, can you bring me a bottle of spray for my dog, two bottles of medicine and the vaccine for the calves? I'll see you at 9.30"

The final distraction, delivering the killer blow to the birthday meal, was a call from a Mark, a cattle farmer, with whom I had spoken earlier in the week. He wanted to discuss a meeting he had been involved with that day. It was about his new building, his management and how his calving was shaping up and he wanted to keep me updated. It is often hard to find enough time for discussions like this during the busy working day, so I didn't mind the call, although Anne did start to roll her eyes when the conversation extended beyond twenty minutes.

"And one final thing," said Mark, as the call drew to a close, "I'd like to invite you, as my guest, to the Boroughbridge Agricultural Society Annual Dinner. It's one of the oldest agricultural societies in the country and it's always a good night. I hope you can come?"

It sounded like a great night out, I just hoped I could negotiate *that* dinner without any interruptions!

Uterine Torsion

"I'm just not happy with her. She looked as if she was going to calve two days ago, so I put her in a pen by herself, just to be quiet. Anyhow, she's not done a thing and now the old girl looks a bit bloated. I know it's late and I don't want to bother you, but I'm just a bit worried."

Whilst the farmer was mildly anxious about his cow, the story he told me late last Saturday night, suggested I would not be seeing the end of my Netflix film for some time.

"Hmm. I'd better come and have a look, Neil. It sounds like it might be something called a uterine torsion". This was my down-the-phone-diagnosis. It was a cold night and I layered up with a coat and a hat as I left the house, although, if I was correct with my assessment, I would not be able to keep my coat on for very long.

By the time I arrived at Neil's farm, he had convinced himself that the situation was much graver than he had initially thought.

"Now I've talked to you, Julian, I'm not at all happy with her. There's something very wrong."

Sure enough, after stripping off my top, applying lubrication to my right arm and feeling gently inside the cow, there was a very obvious clockwise twist of the vagina. My fingers could just about touch the end of one of the calf's hooves. In theory, this dystocia can be relieved by grasping the calf's foot and heroically untwisting the uterus, by rotating the foetus. Sometimes rolling the cow onto her back and using a plank of wood to squash against her tummy can work, or having someone roll the cow, while you try to hold the calf in position. I have to say, I have never had much success with any of these techniques, especially when just the very end of the hoof is all that can be touched. I was unable to get an

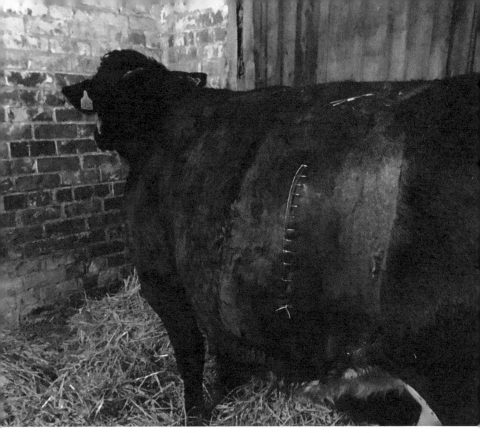

The caesarean went perfectly and the cow was a model patient. It never fails to amaze me how well cows tolerate surgery in a barn!

actual hold on anything that belonged to this calf. A caesarean was required, late this Saturday night.

The cow was persuaded into a suitable position, standing with her right side against a wall and fastened by halter to a perfectly placed metal ring on the wall of the old cowshed. Everything else followed as if on autopilot. I'd done this hundreds of times before, mostly, it seems, at this time of the night; two buckets of warm water, clip hair off the left flank, inject the site with local, scrub and prep the cow, open the surgical kit, first needle threaded with suture material before I start (to save valuable seconds when the abdomen is open and exposed to the straw and cobwebs of the farm), antibiotics and painkillers administered. Finally, I scrubbed my arms and now-bare chest with more antiseptic before unpeeling my scalpel from its packet.

Tonight's operation would be more complicated than a normal caesarean. Once I was into the abdomen, I would need to *untwist* the twisted uterus before I made my incision into its muscular body. It would make the subsequent suturing more straightforward, as the incision would still be facing me, rather than tending to reposition itself back into the depths of the abdomen. The calf was enormous and the surgery was very difficult. At least my patient was perfectly behaved. She only threatened to lift her left hind once and stood still for the duration. Eventually the calf was untwisted and out, landing with a splat on the straw, to everyone's relief.

Stitching up the uterus was next. It's important to make a neat seal but also to be quick. With the cow's insides hanging out of her body, the sooner it is cleaned, closed and put back in its proper place the better.

"I see you've done that a fair few times before!" said Neil, as he admired my suturing.

"Just a few," I replied, and explained that, during my first few months in practise in the North of Scotland, we would do ten of these operations per week.

"Let me know when you're nearly done," added Neil, "I'll ring my wife and ask her to fetch us a cuppa."

So, at nearly one in the morning, it was one of the most delicious cups of tea I could remember for a long time!

Rabbit on the Scales

7th March

Blue was enormous. His ears were even more enormous. Blue was a rabbit; a very big rabbit, and he was sitting quietly in the waiting room with his owner, on a lead just like a dog. The sight took everyone by surprise.

He had come to the practice with another very large rabbit called "Thumper", who was his companion. The supersized lagomorphs were an awesome-looking pair. They were not poorly – they just needed their annual health and weight checks, and to be given their annual vaccinations.

We routinely vaccinate rabbits against two diseases. The most well known is myxomatosis – a horrible disease, that causes a slow and lingering death, with characteristic painful swelling up of the eyes and genitals. So contagious is the disease, that it was introduced to Australia in the 1950s, in an attempt to decimate the wild rabbit population that was displacing the native wildlife. More recently, we have started to vaccinate against a second fatal condition called Rabbit Viral Haemorrhagic Disease. Infection with the VHD virus causes sudden death. Both diseases are rife in the wild rabbit population, so it is crucial, especially in rural areas, that beloved pet rabbits are vaccinated every year to keep them safe.

Just as important for health of a rabbit, is the maintenance of a normal weight and the provision of a suitable diet. We see increasing numbers of overweight rabbits these days, and the associated problems – from a failure to be able to groom properly, to diabetes and urinary tract disease – can all be prevented with dietary management. Research done some years ago by Yorkshire veterinary surgeon, Francis Harcourt-Brown demonstrated that pet rabbits often have much lower bone density than their wild, grass-eating cousins. This weaker bone is a particular problem in the skull, leading to loosening of the teeth and, as a consequence, an

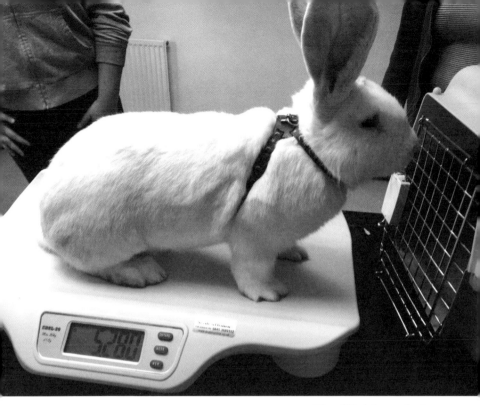

Blue filled the scales!

increased risk of dental disease and, in particular, abscesses associated with the tooth roots. This syndrome is seen most commonly in rabbits fed on muesli style foods – those made up of squashed dried peas, crushed maize and so on. Whilst the whole diet has the correct balance of minerals, rabbits are highly selective feeders and only eat the tasty morsels, leaving the more nutritious bits in the bowl, in much the same way that a young child would avoid the broccoli in favour of the pudding!

The very best diet for a rabbit is grass and hay (good quality feeding hay as opposed to bedding hay, which is often dusty and less palatable: open the bag – good hay smells delicious!) with the addition of a small amount of a complete pelleted food, which gets around the problem of selective grazing. The long fibres in grass and hay are crucial both for even wear of the teeth and for healthy gut function. Occasional treats such as mint, basil or parsley and small branches from an apple or pear tree, complete with leaves make your rabbit's diet perfect.

Thumper hopped onto the scales first. He passed the weight test with flying colours. He was large and robust but not overweight. I peered into his mouth with my 'scope. His back teeth – the molars – were healthy, with uniform wear and no sharp spurs. His front teeth – the incisors – aligned perfectly with no need for any attention either.

Next, we discussed the rabbits' home environment. Stimulating surroundings, to keep a rabbit's mental health robust are just as important as what goes into its food bowl. Tubes to play in, different levels to explore and an outside run that can be moved around on the grass all contribute to a contented life

But Thumper and Blue had everything they needed. Most important of all, they had each other!

Billy with the Broken Hock

14th March

Billy's problem was clear for everyone in the waiting room to see, as the rough coated, fawn coloured lurcher hopped, still wagging his tail, towards the consulting room. The suspicious banana curve of the back part of his lower leg – the bit below the hock – gave me a hefty clue about the likely reason for Billy's lameness.

Mark, his owner, explained what had happened. "Well, he'd been racing around at high speed as usual, then he suddenly stopped and he hasn't put it down since. It happened a few days ago. I thought it might get better if I rested him, but it hasn't. He doesn't look as if he's too bothered, 'cos his tail hasn't stopped wagging, but I think it needs a look at, so I've brought him to see you."

I examined him in some detail, but I knew what had happened. Billy had ruptured the plantar ligaments of his hock – a classic injury when fast dogs overdo it. I could sympathise, having suffered from on-going Achilles tendon injuries at various points through my running and triathlon career. The constant burning sensation within the tendinous tissue is debilitating. In Billy's case, the laxity of the joints demanded an X-ray and would almost certainly require surgical correction.

I arranged with Mark that we would do the X-rays and surgery the following day, after a support bandage and some anti-inflammatories had relieved some of the swelling.

Billy was first on the ops list the next morning and I gathered all the necessary equipment. There are two different ways to fix this injury. One uses a plate on the outside of the hock, with screws to hold it in place, while the second uses a pin, drilled down through the calcaneus (the heel bone) and into the intertarsal joints. This pin is stabilised by wire twisted into the shape of a figure of eight. I took various measurements to decide which option to use. I have

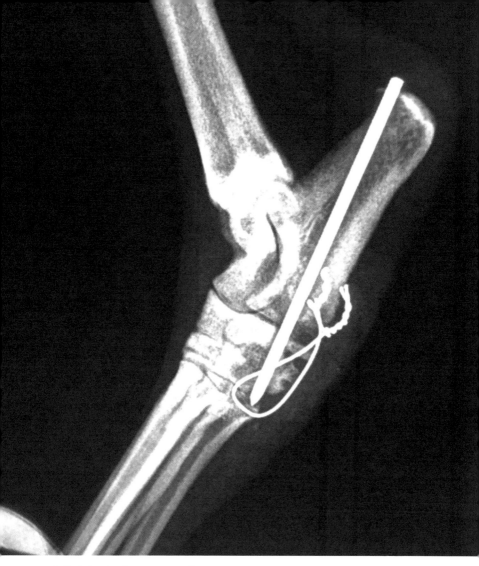

*Billy's hock after surgery. It went
smoothly and was immediately much
more comfortable and very stable.*

done several similar operations recently for the same kind of accident and both methods seem to be of approximately equal merit. Billy was a light, lean dog and, after discussing it with colleagues, who either gave their opinion or had no opinion (in equal proportions) I erred on the side of pin and wire fixation.

I like hock surgery. Whilst there are numerous tiny bones (which can be daunting for a novice surgeon), it is a satisfying joint on which to operate. Usually the injury is serious – when things go wrong in hock, they go REALLY wrong – so the surgery is rewarding. Also, it is an easy part of the body to get at. Cut through the skin and you're straight into the action area. Some orthopaedic surgery involves deep dissection to reach the problem. Give me a hock to repair any day!

Things went well and I had soon found the remains of the plantar ligament. It was completely obliterated as the banana bend and the X-rays had suggested, offering no support whatsoever. I aligned the calcaneus with the rest of the bones and drilled a hole for my pin – always the most tense part of the procedure. Once I had placed the pin, the joint was rock-solid again and I began to relax. I drilled two smaller holes for the wire to pass through, made my figure of eight, tightened it firmly and bent the ends over. So far, so good. I cut and countersunk the pin, so it was flush with the bone, then closed the retinaculum and the skin. Finally, we supported it all in a bandage.

It wasn't long before Billy was awake and lifting his head and his tail was soon wagging again. As I say, I like hock surgery!

Busy Afternoon

21st March

My Friday afternoon appointment list was full, and there were already people waiting, as I rushed in through the side door of the practice, slightly late and with chicken and pesto panini in hand. Wistfully, I left the sandwich to one side, to make a start on afternoon surgery.

Breakfast seemed a distant memory. I had spent the morning repairing a ruptured cruciate ligament in a schnauzer, and treating pneumonic cattle that were coughing in the fog of a winter in the Vale of York. My first patient after what should have been lunch was Daisy. Daisy's owner had already taken her into the consulting room, to await my arrival. Her ear, which had been very sore and inflamed the week before, was looking much better and I waved them both goodbye after administering a final treatment.

"There's a Labrador on its way down," said Fiona, one of the nurses, as soon as I had finished Daisy's check-up. "I think she might have a pyo. Apparently, she's discharging a brown liquid. I thought it would be better to see her now rather than leave her over the weekend."

Fiona, with years of nursing experience, was completely correct and, as I examined Amber later that afternoon, she did indeed show many signs of the serious uterine infection known to dog lovers and veterinary staff as a pyometra. Emma, my colleague, scanned her abdomen as I finished off my appointment list, and then my panini. The scan confirmed our diagnosis of pyometra, and we set about the surgery that would prove to be life saving for Amber.

But before Amber's op was completed, Fiona was back: "Julian, now I've got a horse with colic. It sounds quite urgent and the owners are very worried."

I was already closing the abdomen, so Fiona went back to the phone to reassure the horse's owner that I would be with them in about half an hour. Colic cases are always urgent and necessitate the vet dropping pretty much all other jobs to get there as soon as possible. There was nothing I could do though, before first ensuring Amber was safely off the table and waking up in her kennel. Then, I rushed off. Again.

The horse was at a trekking centre, to which I had not been previously. I made my rapid way down the lane where my sat-nav had taken me and there, waiting in the dusky evening gloom, was a silver coloured pickup. Its owner jumped out as soon as he saw my car headlights.

"Are you Julian? Good, she's down this way. Follow me!" With that, he jumped into his vehicle and sped away down a bumpy track, at about fifty miles an hour, so that I could hardly keep up.

I arrived in the dark yard, pulled up behind the pickup – which, by this time, had either steam or smoke issuing from some part of it – and stepped out of my car, straight into a puddle.

The coloured mare was sweaty and sore and kicking her belly, and was most certainly suffering from colic. Colic is a term to describe abdominal pain and it is a condition that often affects horses. The causes can range from mild, spasmodic colic – easily diagnosed and easily fixed – to severe and life-threatening disease where emergency surgery is the only hope. As I examined the horse with my stethoscope, my left foot squelching from standing in the puddle, the gurgling and squelching noises issuing from the abdomen of my patient confirmed this was spasmodic colic – the least serious type. Horse, owner and vet all breathed a sigh of relief as the spasmolytic drugs coursed their way through her veins. It had been a busy, mixed and varied day – the reason why I love mixed practise.

A New Remedy to an Old Problem

28th March

Dave, the yellow Labrador, limped miserably into my consulting room on Tuesday afternoon. His problem was clear to see, since he couldn't put his right front foot to the ground.

"He's been lame since last weekend and I've had a good look," explained his owner. "I've squeezed his feet and I can't find anything wrong so I thought it was time to bring him to see you, Julian."

I love treating a dog with a human's name!

I examined Dave on the floor – he was too big to lift onto the table. Since our patients can't tell us which bit hurts (if *only* they could talk!), we have to work it out by palpating, squeezing and prodding until there is some sort of reaction. As I felt each pad and probed between Dave's toes, I found a painful, firm swelling. This warranted further exploration under general anaesthetic.

Half an hour later, once I had finished afternoon surgery, we gave Dave his anaesthetic, and I cut over the painful knobble on his foot. There was nothing obvious at first, but after some time exploring the swollen tissue, the most satisfying thing happened. As I squeezed, a large black thorn, almost a centimetre long, shot out of the incision I had made. A couple of sutures and a bandage, were all that was needed and Dave recovered uneventfully in his kennel. It was a painful problem, but one with a simple cure and Dave was soon reunited with his owner. He was also called Dave.

Later that evening, my phone "pinged" with a text message from a colleague.

"Have you any experience of using Red Bull in the treatment of twin lamb in ewes?" said the message on my phone.

It was not a question that I was expecting. I wasn't on duty, but I didn't mind being disturbed. I was intrigued by the new treatment.

"I haven't, but it sounds an interesting idea!" I typed back.

"Twin Lamb Disease" is a condition seen in sheep in the later stages of pregnancy. The lambs grow rapidly in the last few days before being born and quickly use up all the ewe's readily available energy supplies. This energy demand is greater if there is more than one lamb – hence the name "Twin Lamb Disease". The energy deficiency leads the body to try to use its fat reserves. This is fine up to a point and most ewes can cope with it. However, thin sheep that are inadequately nourished, excessively fat sheep with a reduced appetite due to the size of the lambs, or sheep with bad teeth that stop them from eating properly are all at risk. Equally, if late snow covers the fells and the pregnant ewes cannot graze, they can succumb to the disease. In these cases, the fat supplies are relied upon too heavily. This results in a build-up of ketones (which are a by-product of fat metabolism) in the blood stream of the ewe. These ketones can actually suppress the appetite further, as well as causing all sorts of other problems, including blindness. Not being able to see their food makes it even more difficult for affected sheep and they quickly spiral into decline.

There are various remedies that are effective at treating twin lamb disease. Most are based upon the use of energy drinks to provide instant glucose, so it was easy to see why the farmer, desperate to fix his poorly ewe and save her lambs, would reach for a can of something special. I had, however, never heard of adding caffeine.

"How did it work?" I had to ask, later in the evening. The reply came back quickly.

"Well. It didn't exactly give her wings. It actually gave the poor sheep explosive diarrhoea…"

Maybe the old remedies are the best after all!

Ski Mountaineering in Switzerland and Caesareans in Sutton

5th April

It was back to veterinary earth with a bump when I walked into work at the start of the week. I hadn't even taken my coat off when Marion rushed up to tell me there was a heifer to calve.

"As soon as possible, they said. They're very worried. It's a heifer and the one that calved yesterday was very tight and ended up quite badly bruised. You'd better take the Caesar kit!"

I headed straight out of the door, with only moments to say good morning to everyone before heading up to Sutton-under-Whitestonecliffe with a camera crew in tow. The camera crew always follow when a case looks as if it will be interesting or exciting.

As I drove to the farm, I gathered my thoughts. I had spent the last four days in the Alps as part of a team participating in a ski mountaineering race. Ski mountaineering uses special skis and boots, and "skins" which are applied to the bottom of the skis so that they grip the snow when climbing up steep slopes. I love it. The pioneering feeling of ascending a remote alpine summit on skis followed by the thrill of skiing down, off-piste, negotiating rocks, trees and cliffs is the perfect antidote to the busy life of a veterinary surgeon.

The race took us up and over a mountain called the Steghorn, in the Bernese Oberland and it involved 3000m of ascent over a distance of about 36 kilometres. After just an hour of racing, at about five in the morning and on the first major climb of the massive route that lay ahead I had a major calamity. As I tried to remove a ball of snow from the bottom of one of my skis, I managed to snap one of my new and very expensive, lightweight ski poles. I was completely snookered with only one pole. Facing the prospect of abandoning the race I had spent months working towards, I searched around in the dark for something I could use as a substitute. After an abortive attempt at using a discarded flagpole, I managed to find a suitable stand-in. The wooden staff – which looked just like an alpenstock – was not very good to say the least, and very much worse than the carbon fibre poles being used by all the other competitors, but at least I could complete the course with the rest of my team, albeit with rather less style.

At the summit of the Steghorn (over 3100m) it was windy, icy and a very cold –15 degrees Celsius, and I was up there with one ski pole and a long wooden stick. I could hardly have been further away from calving a heifer in a cowshed in North Yorkshire.

But I love calving a heifer just as much I love scaling an alp and so, on Monday morning, I raced off to Sutton with great enthusiasm. The heifer was young and the calf was big. Its feet were crossed suspiciously as they emerged from the birth canal, suggesting a tight squeeze. It didn't take me long to realise that the calf was too big, and the only way it could be delivered would be by caesarean section, as Marion and the farmer had predicted. The op went well, despite the first-time mother being less than thrilled by my intervention. She spent the duration of the op trying to manoeuvre herself into various difficult positions that made things awkward. She will do well though, once the wound has healed.

And the calf?

By the time I had finished suturing its mother's skin, it had wobbled to its feet and was trying to walk, as unsteady as I was as I skied down the Steghorn clutching my wooden ski pole. I could sympathise with its plight!

Lambing

12th April

Lambing time is well and truly upon us in Thirsk. In fact, it has really been upon us since January. Located as we are, in the Vale of York but on the edge of the North York Moors, the practice looks after a mixture of upland and lowland flocks. Many of the lowland flocks have finished lambing already, but the upland farms are right in the middle of this, the busiest period of their farming year. For those that keep sheep, lambing time is concentrated over about a month and a half. During this period there is very little sleep for the shepherd, as every birth is supervised and every lamb nurtured to give it the best possible start. Since all sheep farms lamb their flocks at slightly different times, the veterinary surgeons at the practice have lambings and lambing related ailments to deal with all the way through from the cold and dark of early January, to the warm spring days at the end of April. This is a good thing though, because all vets like lambing sheep.

I was called out on Wednesday afternoon to see a lambing ewe, on a farm just outside Kepwick, on the edge of the Hambleton Hills.

"I can't make nothing of her, Julian," Arthur explained when I arrived. "I've got the first one out, but I'm buggered if I can get the other one!"

This was very unusual, because as every experienced shepherd or veterinary surgeon knows, it is usually the first lamb that is the hardest to deliver. Nothing was ever straightforward though, when I came to see Arthur and his sheep.

Arthur was kicking himself when, after just a few minutes, the second healthy but meconium-stained lamb was flapping its ears in the straw next to the first-born. The lamb's head had been twisted back against its shoulder, rather than being lined up with its front feet, and Arthur had been trying to sort it out using his new plastic lambing aid.

"You're better off just using your hands, Arthur!" I explained.

I could never make anything of these plastic lambing aids either, and Arthur chucked his device into the corner of the lambing shed in disgust.

The lambing had been simple enough, but Arthur was determined to get his money's worth out of my visit. There was no chance I could unpeel my waterproof trousers and climb out of my wellies just yet!

"While you're here, could you just have a quick look at this ewe?"

Often, the *while-you're-here* jobs are more involved and more challenging than the original emergency.

"She has a prolapse," Arthur explained and then paused, before continuing. "Actually, I have two sheep, both with prolapses. You'd better have a look at both of 'em."

Both sheep had yet to lamb and both had developed vaginal prolapses. These can be serious, but often are straightforward to manage with a simple device called a "retainer". Another bit of plastic, this time shaped like a spoon, a retainer fits snuggly inside the vagina and is fastened in place using bailer twine, either tied to the adjacent fleece, or to a collar around the sheep's neck (it's not very glamorous being a sheep!). Both these prolapses, however, were well and truly beyond the plastic spoon stage and certainly in need of some veterinary intervention. Half an hour later, both were replaced and the outlook for the two ewes and their yet-to-be-born lambs was considerably better.

I still wasn't quite finished though. Just as I was about to leave, Arthur's daughter came rushing out of the lambing shed.

"You couldn't just have a look at this lamb could you? I think there's something wrong with its navel…"

Like I said, lambing time can be a long and drawn out affair.

Easter

19th April

Easter weekend is a busy one for veterinary surgeons, but the calls and duties are shared out equally, so we can all have some time off with our families. My wife, Anne, had heard from a friend that there was a colony of common and grey seals beneath the cliffs at Ravenscar so, on Good Friday, armed with cameras and hoping that the mist and rain would keep the crowds at bay, we went to investigate.

After a short walk across the gorse-clad cliff top, we could see the rocky shore below. The rocks were grey and so was the sea and we could see no seals at all. Maybe they had gone back to sea?

However, as we scrambled down the steep path that wound down to the sea, it was just possible to make out a handful of slug-like forms scattered amongst the rocks. They were definitely seals but they looked as if they had been stranded and left behind. Five minutes further down the path though, it became clear that these few were just the outliers. There was a huge herd (or "rookery", according to the dictionary, although that seems a bit silly, as they were seals and not rooks) of about fifty seals, relaxing, yawning and scratching themselves, with the odd skirmish here and there. We sat on a rock for a while and watched these fascinating wild animals, who were utterly unperturbed by our presence.

Back at the surgery, it was another a hectic week. Lambing and calving is still in full swing, and with the start of the new series of *The Yorkshire Vet*, there was also all the promotional stuff to do. I think I am getting better at radio interviews, but they still put me some way outside my comfort zone. My appointment at BBC Radio York was a very relaxed affair as I talked about the opening story of the first episode – the case of Dobby the llama, with his fractured jaw.

I see quite a few camelids (llamas and alpacas) these days. The first herd we treated arrived in the village of Sutton-Under-Whitestonecliffe in the aftermath of the Foot and Mouth crisis. The farm had lost all its dairy cows to the cull, and the family, with no cows to milk, had done what they had never chance to do before, and gone on holiday to South America. Soon after they returned home, brimming with the excitement of discovering this new species, they filled the fields that were once home to black and white cows, with alpacas.

Alpacas are fascinating creatures, quite different to the cows and sheep we are used to in rural North Yorkshire. I have gradually learnt about the diseases and veterinary conditions to which they are prone, and their curious and gentle nature has completely captivated me.

Llamas are slightly more feisty than alpacas but similar to treat and just as entertaining to deal with. Some weeks ago, I was called to see Dobby, who had made a nasty mess of his jaw. Half of his front teeth were hanging off, along with the bit of bone to which they were attached. With the injection of some local anaesthetic, I managed to wire the fragment back into alignment, but it meant four weeks of solitary confinement for poor Dobby and he wasn't amused. The fracture healed nicely though, and I was there to see him reunited with his friends, back out in the field. The joy he felt was plain to see as he bounced around the hillside like a springbok. It was a perfect reward for all our efforts.

Farming in Yorkshire has changed dramatically in the twenty years since I have been a vet, but it can only survive if the next generation is inspired. Maybe these unusual species can go some way towards achieving this.

Calving and Lambing at Sutton

26th April

As I drove up towards Sutton Bank I passed an ambulance, speeding in the opposite direction with its blue lights flashing. Since it was after midnight, there was little need for the lights to flash as, apart from me, there were no other cars around, but it reminded me that I was not the only person dealing with emergencies this evening.

When I arrived at the farm to see the heifer, which was struggling to calve, Victoria, the farmer's daughter, was waiting for me, hopping from foot to foot.

"Oh, thank you for coming so quickly," she said, clearly upset. "It's a nightmare. This heifer is calving and James has just been rushed to hospital. She came at him when he went in to check her and he got squashed against the wall and banged his head. He passed out and that's when Dad called me to come and help. They are on their way to hospital now, so you and I are in charge of the heifer!"

The ambulance I had passed had been rushing the injured James to A&E. It was a stark reminder of just how dangerous it can be dealing with cattle.

Luckily for me the Limousin-cross heifer was, by now, safely fastened in the cattle crush. It was a big calf and very tight so I needed the help of a calving jack, but all went smoothly and it wasn't long before it was spluttering its first breaths in the straw, the new mother instinctively licking it dry and coaxing it to its feet. As I cleaned my wellies under an outside light, surrounded by the pitch black of the early hours, I knew that I would soon be back in bed, unlike poor Victoria, who would be on her way up to the James Cook hospital.

Sadly, my time back in bed was only short-lived. At 3am I was woken again by the persistent beep of my pager. There was a sheep to lamb – she'd been messing about for six hours and nothing had happened. I made my way back along the road to Sutton Bank for the second time in three hours. There were no ambulances this time, but the plight of the enormous Suffolk ewe was every bit as much of an emergency as my previous call. She was suffering from a condition called "ring-womb", whereby the cervix fails to dilate properly, obstructing the birth canal. This is a bad thing to have at 3am, because the only way to deal with it is by slow, patient dilation of the cervix using a gentle hand. It cannot be rushed and the whole process can take quite some time. The farmer (whose name was Janet) and I were as relieved as the Suffolk was, when I had finally managed to correct the ring womb and two healthy lambs were delivered, just as the first glimmer of daylight started to appear.

Nights like this are always tough, as we are straight back to work in the morning and there is rarely any opportunity to catch up on the lost sleep. Driving home from Janet's farm though, I still felt the almost immeasurable satisfaction of bringing new life into the world. Even after twenty years of doing this, the thrill never gets less.

Janet called into the practice the next morning to report that all was well with ewe and lambs. I phoned Victoria to check on everyone's health – human and bovine. James had been discharged from hospital after CT scans, pelvic braces and lots of morphine. Thankfully there were no major breaks. The heifer and her calf were both doing well too! It had been a tough night for us all!

Tour de Yorkshire

3rd May

It all seemed to be happening last weekend. The fun started on Friday evening. I was on second call for Matt, one of our young and enthusiastic veterinary surgeons. He had been called to a heifer struggling to calve. She had been bulled by accident when she was a bit too young and, when he saw her small stature, Matt knew she would never be able to deliver the calf naturally. He needed to do a caesarean and called me in to help. We always have two vets on call at night and during the weekend for just such eventualities. Some jobs are much easier with two pairs of hands.

We are fortunate at the moment to have a superb team of veterinary surgeons. There are the old hands (sadly, that now includes me), and a couple of vets, each with eight or more years experience under their belts. We also have three younger vets who have the advantage of youth, vigour and unbridled enthusiasm (not that the rest of us are not enthusiastic – it's the youth and vigour that wane with the years!). It is a great balance. As I arrived at the farm and donned my wellies, I knew that Matt would be raring to go. He had already clipped the heifer's left flank, numbed the op site with local anaesthetic and prepped it ready for surgery. She was lying comfortably in the straw, so we were loathed to get her up, even though it is much easier to perform a bovine "section" with the animal standing.

Matt did a great job. All I really needed to do was to offer moral support. A healthy Aberdeen Angus calf was soon wobbling to its feet. We always try to finish the operation before the calf starts tottering around in search of milk from the mother's udder.

We had another caesarean later in the weekend, but this time on a little bitch. More healthy babies. Three little pups are every bit as satisfying as one large calf!

For me, though, the highlight of the weekend came on Sunday morning. I was woken by the "beep beep", not of another emergency call, but of my alarm clock. Rising at any time with a "five" in the title is never exactly fun, but it was a beautiful morning. I had arranged for a colleague to stand in for me on second call while I headed to Fox Valley, to ride the Maserati Tour de Yorkshire Sportive with a group of friends. The one-hundred hilly kilometres around South and West Yorkshire shared some of the same route as the pros, who were riding the last leg of the three-day Tour de Yorkshire.

Some of the route was familiar territory for me. I knew the hills around Emley Moor and Penistone from my childhood, and I was looking forward to the ride, although I knew that not one of the hills would match the challenge of Sutton or Boltby Banks, which were on my doorstep in Thirsk.

It was a great and very successful day's ride, with nearly five thousand other cyclists. Even at half past eight in the morning, there were crowds out on the roadsides, cheering on the riders. Yorkshire was once again at its brilliant best!

As I waited for my mates at the end of the ride (I had left them behind on the first climb up Pea Royd Lane – it was steep, but not a patch on Boltby Bank) I chatted to a fellow finisher. He had a red face but had loved every minute.

"It was brilliant – what a day!" he spluttered, catching his breath as he crossed the finish line. "But way too hilly for me. We don't have this sort of thing in Essex!"

All I could say in reply was, "Welcome to Yorkshire!"

Suki and I became very close during her chemotherapy treatment – another reason why this kind of case is so rewarding.

Suki the Schnauzer

10th May

I knew all about Suki before she came to surgery for the first time. The little, black schnauzer was suffering from a type of cancer called lymphoma. Sadly, we see this condition, which affects the lymph nodes, quite frequently in our canine patients. It is comparable to leukaemia in humans, and can have similarly devastating implications for both the patient and their family. However, it often responds very well to chemotherapy, and this is where my involvement began.

Suki had been a patient of my wife Anne, who is also a veterinary surgeon. But Anne was moving to a new job, and both she and Suki's owners were worried that there was no one experienced in the use of chemotherapy to continue Suki's treatment. This is one of my main areas of interest so, when Anne asked me, I was only too glad to be able to help. There is sometimes a reluctance to use chemotherapy in pets, but this is misplaced. The drugs are well tolerated and straightforward to administer. The hair loss and terrible sickness seen in people does not occur in dogs to anything like the same extent, and they are, more often than not, back to their normal pre-lymphoma selves within a couple of days of starting treatment.

On Suki's first visit to see me, Anne came into the clinic to make sure the handover was smooth and that everyone was happy with the new arrangement. Suki had been one of her favourite patients and I could immediately tell why. The little dog stumped happily across the waiting room, oblivious to her illness. The only tell-tale sign, when I examined her, was the enlarged lymph node in front of her right shoulder. It refused to follow the orders of the strict chemotherapy regime and, unlike all her other lymph nodes, which had shrunk as hoped, it was still the size of a prize-winning conker.

Every day Suki needed an array of tablets, along with an

intravenous injection once every three weeks, to control the lymphoma. There is a delicate balance to be struck between treating the cancer cells vigorously enough to halt the progress of the disease, and not having too severe an effect upon the normal body cells. The bone marrow is the most vulnerable, which is a pain in the neck, because the bone marrow makes all the important blood cells. Managing cancer patients can be difficult.

The best bit of treating these cases though, is the amazing relationship that develops between the vet and the nurse, and the dog and its owners. From that first, terrible diagnosis and the decision upon whether to embark upon treatment (it is not appropriate in all cases), through the anxious wait to see if the medication is working and the ongoing fine-tuning to balance beneficial effects against deleterious ones, we get to know the owners very closely. But the dog, who willingly and with total trust, trots in to see us, week after week, always secures a very special place in our affections.

As soon as the schnauzer came into my room, her short tail started wagging and her eyes lit up. I'm sure some dogs realise that we are trying to help them and Suki almost held out her front leg for me to give the injection that would probably make her feel rubbish for the next few days.

She lifted her head up to look at me, quite content that I was doing the best thing for her.

"Well done, Suki," I said, as I peeled off the protective gloves and gown that are essential attire when handling cytotoxic drugs. "Is she always this good?"

"Oh yes! She's a very good girl is my Suki." Her mum ruffled her ears.

I made another appointment for three weeks' time, and waved them goodbye. I knew I had found a friend with whom I could join a journey. Hopefully it would have a happy destination.

TB Testing

17th May

I have been TB testing cattle this week. It is not something I do very often nowadays.

TB testing used to be a regular job for all mixed and farm practices. We were required (and paid) by DEFRA, to test all the herds looked after by the practice. The interval between tests depended upon the incidence of TB in the area. We are lucky in Yorkshire to have a very low level of TB, so (under normal circumstances) animals only need to be tested every four years. This is in huge contrast to some parts of the country, where the disease is rife and all stock must be tested annually. It is a fairly mundane task, but important, and has always provided a good opportunity to catch up with the farmer and get a sense of how things are going on the farm.

However, recently there have been some dramatic changes. Three years ago, the job of TB testing the nation's cows was put out to tender by the government. The company that won the contract (which was made up of a national consortium of veterinary practices) decided that, instead of employing its own TB testers – which would have required quite some effort and expense – it would offer the job back to practising vets, who had been doing the job for the last sixty years. The only difference was, that they expected us to do it for a rate of pay somewhat lower than the minimum wage. Needless to say, we respectfully declined.

Some farmers though, still prefer to have their own vet to TB test their animals, and are happy to arrange for us to carry out the task privately. This was the case for the two herds I saw this week. One of them had some post-movement tests to undertake – to make sure cattle that had just been moved onto the premises did not have TB, before introducing them to the rest of the herd. The other herd was under movement restriction, after there had been a suspicious case at a neighbouring farm. It was a tense few days, doing the tests and awaiting the results.

TB testing itself has not altered since the 1940s. It relies on injecting small amounts of avian and bovine tuberculin into the skin on the neck of each cow. Three days later, any lumps that have developed are measured. The size of the avian lump relative to the bovine lump determines whether the animal is a reactor, an inconclusive reactor or free from TB. We are told by DEFRA that this remains the most accurate and sensitive of tests, although in the twenty-first century, when massive advances have been made in both diagnosis of, and screening for, disease, it seems peculiar still to be relying on a test developed in the 1930s. But ours is not to reason why. Ours is just to test.

But we can't just test. The new regime requires that we revalidate our skills (a twenty-first century term if ever there was one), so I enrolled on the obligatory course. Before I could embark upon the ten hours of reading, write the reports of previous tests, and carry out the supervised test to confirm I could still do the thing I have been doing every few weeks for the last twenty years, I had to complete a preliminary exam.

It will not divulge too many secrets to say that the answer to the question,

"Where should you dispose of your bucket of disinfectant after cleaning your wellies?" is not

a) down the drain, or *b) onto the concrete*, but actually and surprisingly *c) into the bushes*!

I failed that part.

The rest of my questions were more conventional and I think I got most of them right. I have done everything I need to do, and now I am ready to sit my final exam. But first I need to go back to check my cattle for lumps. It is not just me that is hoping for a clear test.

Cows don't really like being TB tested and a modern, well designed cattle crush makes the job much easier.

The Cat that was "Just Not"

Beryl was a boy. This was the first thing that his owners explained, as I tried to persuade the reluctant and misnamed cat out of his basket. As I grappled with Beryl, I asked my usual questions, starting with, "How is Beryl today?"

The first half of the answer came quickly, "He's just not…" I waited for the rest of the story, but nothing was forthcoming.

"He's just not what?" I asked, searching for more information about the cat, who was sitting quietly on the table, not giving any clues about the reason for his visit.

"…moving very quickly," was the rest of the information, when it eventually arrived.

"He's lost his…*fluidity,* you see." I understood what was meant by this very non-specific description of Beryl's illness, but it was not very helpful. A lugubrious cat is a diagnostic challenge. His appetite was okay, his toilet habits unknown ("he goes outside, in the bushes, you see.")

Luckily for me, my stethoscope identified a sore throat and my thermometer identified a temperature of 104 degrees. Beryl was certainly poorly, and I made a tentative diagnosis of laryngitis. I gave him some treatment and asked to see him again the following day, to check his progress. Although my diagnosis was by no means certain, I felt confident my injections would be helpful.

My next patient, a five-year-old whippet called Dora, was on her holidays. She had become ill on the way to Yorkshire from Lincolnshire and was showing exactly the same signs as Beryl – standing still and not moving at all, let alone not very quickly. Her temperature was exactly the same as Beryl's too, 104 degrees. The answers to my questions were more helpful this time. It turned out that Dora had been in season just three weeks previously. I was immediately suspicious that she was suffering from a condition called "pyometra". This is a serious infection of the uterus, whereby the uterine horns, each usually about the diameter and size of a pencil, fill up with pus, becoming distended so that they resemble two Cumberland sausages. There is a high risk both of rupture of the uterus, and of life threatening toxaemia from the infection.

I reached for the ultrasound scanner to confirm the diagnosis; sure enough loops of distended, fluid-filled uterus where visible on the screen. Dora had a pyometra and needed surgery immediately. I sent her owner off to explore the pleasant market towns of North Yorkshire, promising to phone with an update as soon as I could. Within quarter of an hour, Dora was anaesthetised, clipped and prepped and in theatre. The procedure was exactly the same as a "spay" operation – that is to say, an ovariohysterectomy. I ligated both Dora's ovaries and carefully removed her distended uterus. Its blood vessels were engorged and its walls stretched perilously thin, risking catastrophic rupture at any point. She had arrived in North Yorkshire just in time.

Avoidance of this serious, but common condition is one of the reasons we advise owners to spay non-breeding bitches when they are young. Whilst removing a pyometra is in principle just a spay, operating on a sick and compromised patient is many times more challenging, and brings with it a significant risk of life threatening complications.

However, for Dora, everything went very smoothly during her time in theatre and, before long, I was on the phone to her owner, reassuring her that her little whippet would be fine.

"I'm just having a lovely cup of coffee," she said, relief in her voice, "I'll come and get her in half an hour, if that's OK?"

Not bad service, I thought.

Mangalitzas on the Move

31st May

Last week, I met a lovely couple who had come to stay near Thirsk. Clara and Hal were from Holland, and they had travelled through the night to get to our lovely part of North Yorkshire. They were beautiful individuals, with wonderful, thick, curly blond hair. The hair was all over their bodies, which was unusual for a pig, but these were "hairy pigs" – a rare breed called the "Mangalitza".

Mangalitza pigs originate from Hungary and are derived from a cross between a wild boar and a breed of pig from Serbia. Twenty years ago there were just two hundred of these extraordinary pigs left in Eastern Europe, but a few enthusiasts have taken up their cause. The meat they produce is marbled, which means fat is engrained throughout it. This gives a wonderful, rich flavour, more akin to beef than the ultra-lean, but often insipid pork that is more commonly available now. The fat, apparently, has special, life-enhancing properties as it contains relatively high levels of cholesterol-busting monounsaturated fats and omega fatty acids. Mangalitza pork has become popular in swanky restaurants and I can confirm that it tastes delicious.

But it is not the omega fatty acids in the meat that make heads turn. These pigs are remarkable because, at first sight, they look just like sheep. Their thick, curly hair looks like wool. So, a herd of them, roaming freely in an electric-fenced paddock, looks more like a flock.

My presence was required to take DNA samples from the pigs, to confirm their identities. Hal, the boar, was destined to father a whole generation of piglets on Lisa's farm, so his genetic provenance was important, given the small gene pool of the breed. This was why these two had come all the way from Holland – to try to expand the gene pool and avoid in-breeding.

Hal was a Mangalitza pig, all the way from Holland, providing a much needed injection of new DNA for this rare breed of pig.

The pigs arrived in the most luxurious animal transporter I have ever seen. It was deep in shavings, immaculately clean and even had air conditioning. The haulier lowered the tailgate, and the pair waddled calmly down the ramp, to make their new home near Helmsley. I knew they would enjoy a great life. Once Hal had recovered from the journey he would be straight into action, fathering piglets and expanding the herd.

The pig work in our practice has changed considerably over the years. Most large pig units are looked after by specialist pig vets, whose role is more to oversee the health of the herd than to treat the individual. Our porcine patients, however, typically live on small farms and are often rare breeds, which results in a very different type of veterinary involvement. Indeed, we mostly *are* treating the individual, which brings with it new challenges – especially when those individuals aren't so keen on being treated by a vet.

This was certainly the case with "Monica", the first of Lisa's Mangalitza pigs I encountered. She had recently farrowed, and had stopped eating. She had even refused melon, which was her favourite food, so clearly something was amiss. Unfortunately, she was also ferociously protective of her babies and had big, sharp tusks. I had zero chance of getting close enough to perform a proper examination, so I decided to inject the bad tempered sow using a special lance, which would put some distance between her teeth and me. As I released the plunger, Monica leapt up and charged, fully intent on protecting her babies from the intruder in her pigsty. Instinctively I let out a scream, of girl-like proportions, as I fled from the pen – straight towards the cameras, filming for *The Yorkshire Vet*, who had come along to capture the story of the amazing hairy pig. Despite my protestations at the inclusion of this clip in an episode, I knew that a screaming vet running away from a charging Mangalitza would be sure to make the edit!

Massive Eye

7th June

Richard called at the practice on Wednesday morning. He was worried about one of his recently acquired bullocks. He had bought the batch of cattle a few days previously and, as they settled in to their new surroundings, he had noticed that one had a very swollen eye.

"I've looked it up on YouTube," he told me. "And I wonder whether it might need to be removed?"

"How times have changed!" I thought to myself.

Farmers know their stock very well and it is not uncommon for them to have reached a diagnosis and come up with a plan for treatment some time before the veterinary surgeon arrives. Our small animal clients frequently turn to Dr Google for answers (sometimes rushing in with their pet, convinced it is suffering from a condition that has only been documented twice – in wild dogs in Peru) but this was the first time a farmer had presented me with a solution found on YouTube.

"I'll come up and have a look if you'd like?" I offered.

It was a sunny day and a visit up to the Hambleton hills was a much better prospect than the large pile of mundane practice admin that really needed my attention. I thought it was unlikely that the eye would need to be removed. It is not a common procedure in cattle (unless you are a vet in New Zealand, apparently, where they have a special implement – a bit like a grapefruit spoon – which is designed especially for the job). I had only done the operation once before, in an effort to remove a tumour that was invading around the eyelids of a Hereford cow. It was many years ago and, as I recall, it did not go particularly well. There was blood everywhere and the tumour was much deeper seated than I had expected. I wasn't in a rush to repeat the experience.

When I arrived at the farm, the black and white Friesian was standing patiently in the cattle crush, quite unperturbed by the enormous protrusion that was its right eye. I couldn't quite believe what I was looking at. The eyeball was of joke-shop proportions and was bulging alarmingly. The technical term for an eyeball that is swollen beyond its normal size is "Buphthalmos". It derives from the Greek word "Ox eye" and could not have been more apposite.

I prodded and probed the eye to work out the best course of action. There was clearly no vision at all and the edges of the cornea – the surface layer – were distended to the point where rupture was an imminent possibility. A ruptured eyeball would be a disaster.

It was tempting to agree with Richard and his search engine that the eye needed to be removed. But the removal of any part of the body is not something to take lightly. It is always a last resort. I pulled various faces, just like a builder who is making an estimate for a complicated bit of work – not because I thought this would be an expensive procedure, but simply because I was trying to think through all the options.

After lengthy deliberations, I suggested to Richard that we try a more conservative approach in the first instance. I would give two steroid injections into the eye with the hope and intention that the swelling would recede. For all its gruesome appearance, it was hard to say that the bullock was actually in a lot of pain or discomfort, and this way it might be possible to avoid some fairly major surgery. We both felt the simple approach, at this point in proceedings, was the correct one. I administered the medication and arranged to call back next week. Watch this space…

Opposite: The bullock's eye looked like something from a joke shop, but it must surely have been very painful.

Back to Richard's Farm

Exactly a week after my first visit to see the case of the bullock-with-the-massive-eye, Richard called back at the practice to give an update.

"It's just the same, Julian," he reported. "No better, no worse. What shall we do? I've been keeping a close watch on him over the last week. He eats and gets on alright, but he definitely can't see anything out of that eye."

It was the news that, deep down, I had expected, even though I had hoped it would not be the case. I mulled over the options.

"Is it watering at all?" I asked.

"Yes, it is actually," Richard confirmed. "There's always a trickle of water out of the corner."

This was vital information. Excessive lacrimation is a sign of pain in an eye – imagine how your eye waters when you get grit behind a contact lens. On top of the risk that the eyeball would rupture, the animal was experiencing increased pain.

"We'd better have it out," I said, with bold conviction.

"When can you come?" asked Richard. "I'm busy tomorrow but I can have him in the crush in an hour's time if you can fit it in."

By strange coincidence, an eye operation scheduled for that morning, on one of my canine patients, had just been cancelled so I could simply swap my canine patient for a bovine one, and so we made our plan.

There were two important jobs to do before I set off for the farm:

First, research how to provide adequate local anaesthesia for the operation – in our small animal patients we always do this procedure under general anaesthetic, but this was not an option for

Amazingly, the surgery to enucleate the diseased eye was very straightforward and the bullock recovered very quickly.

the bullock, as general anaesthetics in cattle are fraught with risk and complication.

Second, find the camera crew.

The latter was easy – Laura and Rory were on the scene in seconds. They knew that this had the makings of an amazing story for *The Yorkshire Vet*.

The former was a bit more involved. I had to decide between the Petersson block, which involved a six-inch long, slightly curved needle, or the Four Point Retrobulbar Block. The fact that the practice did not have any six-inch long, slightly curved needles made the decision considerably easier, and I was soon on my way.

The bullock was, again, waiting patiently in the crush when I arrived. The eye looked exactly the same as it had the previous week, with the addition of a watery discharge from the inside corner. The main difference was that I now had a large collection of onlookers all eager to observe the spectacle, which did little to quell my mild anxiety.

The four point retrobulbar block worked a treat – I injected slightly more local in each site than the recommended 10mls, just to be sure, and I was ready to go. So was Felicity, Richard's wife, who was on her way to a birthday treat at a local spa. A friend had arrived to collect the birthday girl, just as I made my first incision. I glanced up from the operating site.

Both ladies were wearing pretty summer dresses: "You might want to stand a little bit further back," I suggested. I knew there was the potential for blood spurting great distances. A blood-spattered dress wouldn't make a good start to a day at the spa.

"We'd better go," said the friend. "We don't want to be late."

She was either genuinely anxious about being late or keen to avoid the gruesome sight in the barn.

"I'm not going anywhere yet," objected Felicity. "Not 'til I've seen what happens with this eye. It's amazing!"

The op went perfectly. After an hour of surgery, the Friesian was happily munching silage as if nothing had happened. It really *was* amazing. As Felicity and her friend headed off to the spa, I could only imagine the conversations that would unfold as the masseurs did their stuff and made the customary small talk.

All Creatures Great and Small

21st June

My night on call set the tone for a busy day ahead. I was woken by my pager in the early hours, summoning me to a pony suffering from colic. Colic is the word used to describe abdominal pain, and is a common problem in horses. The equine bowel is an accident waiting to happen, long and tortuous as it is. Colic can be very serious, even life threatening, but luckily for Dotty the Shetland pony, her colic was simple to deal with – an intravenous injection of an antispasmodic drug to stop her cramping pains was all that was required.

A twenty-year-old cat, unable to stand, was the next patient to break my sleep. Sadly, there was no magic injection to cure the march of old age. I hadn't been home long, and was just making a cup of tea, as the rest of the family started to stir, when another call came in, this time to see a sick calf whose story had a happier ending.

"It's the one you came to see a couple of months ago," explained Mike. "It had pneumonia then, but now it's laid out. I fetched him in with his mother last night. The weather was bad – and so is this calf."

An urgent call like this, at the time of the morning when everyone needs to get to school and work, presents a logistical problem in our household. However, with some minor juggling, everybody, including me, ended up in the right place at the correct time.

The young Beef Shorthorn was in a lot of pain. His bloated abdomen was as tight as a drum. Bloat can be rapidly fatal if the pressure is not relieved quickly. I cleaned and numbed an area on the left flank, so I could insert a device called a trochar-and-cannula. As the pointy tube entered the rumen, the satisfying hiss of escaping gas told me that this little calf would be fine. Its

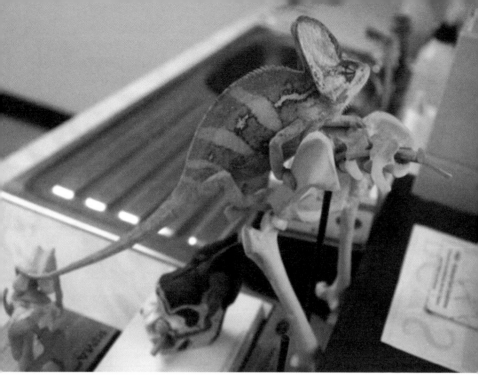

A chameleon is one of the more unusual patients I get to see, even in very varied mixed practise. This one is sitting on a plastic model of a dog's hip.

abdomen deflated like a burst balloon, and soon resumed its normal proportions. After stitching the tube in place to allow the rumen to recover, I said farewell to Mike and headed back to the practice to see an anaemic bloodhound puppy called Rudie. Anaemia in a bloodhound somehow seemed a contradiction in terms!

After a house visit to vaccinate nine cats, it was time for afternoon surgery. One of my patients was Emerald, a young female chameleon. Her new owner had rushed her to the surgery, having found her lying in the bottom of the tank. She thought Emerald was dead. By the time they arrived, however, the chameleon had revived and, as we discussed her problems, she slowly made her way up my arm onto my shoulder and sat on my head.

In exotic species, health problems often arise as a result of issues with their husbandry. Emerald was suffering from dehydration. After some detective work, it transpired that the foliage in her tank was wrong. In fact, it wasn't transpiring at all, which was the problem. Chameleons cannot drink water in the conventional way and rely on imbibing moisture from the surface of leaves. The plastic leaves in Emerald's tank did not hold sufficient water. Again, no magic injections were needed, just a change of foliage.

My next client was flustered. "I'm sorry, Julian. Eric and Charlie need their nails cutting and Charlie needs his blood test." Nothing unusual so far. "The problem is, I'm due a conference call with work in thirty seconds. Do you mind if I take it?"

I agreed to clip the nails and take the blood in complete silence, but the next ten minutes was very odd:

"Thank you all for joining me today. I know you're all busy, but Steven has some questions about the costings for the branch restructuring…Well, yes, but most of the IT costs, hardwear and so on are accounted for centrally and the local networking costs can be offset. The lead time is short so we can source them at short notice…"

It all sounded a million miles away from my day. I was happy to be kneeling on the floor, clipping a greyhound's toenails.

Antifreeze Toxicity

28th June

My night on call this week was Thursday. As evening surgery was drawing to a close, there was a phone call from a worried farmer. A calf had come down with pneumonia. I went immediately, with Laura and Rory, one of the camera crews, in tow. Pneumonia in cattle can be fatal so prompt action was essential. Fortunately, the calf was not too sick, so having given it some treatment I headed for home, while Laura and Rory went in search of sustenance in the supermarket.

However, they had to abandon their shopping basket before the check out, as another call came in. A cat had returned from her day's adventures with a large laceration on her tummy. This was quickly followed by a Jack Russell terrier who had been hit by a car. My pager just kept bleeping. The last message was about Lottie the Staffie. She had drunk some antifreeze. This was a very serious problem and not one I would have expected on a warm summer evening.

"You'd better come straight down," I said to the worried owner.

It was nearly nine o'clock in the evening but the waiting room was busier than it had been during afternoon surgery. The cat needed to be stitched up, the Jack Russell needed some X-rays and Lottie needed urgent attention to stop her from succumbing to the effects of ethylene glycol toxicity (this is the active ingredient of antifreeze). I quickly assessed all the cases. It was clear I needed to deal with Lottie first.

We see antifreeze poisoning every so often, usually in winter, and most frequently in cats, who like to lap the sweet liquid screen wash that has dribbled out of car windscreen washers. It causes rapid and severe kidney damage. Lottie's owner explained what had happened:

"I'd been draining the radiator of my van and there was about half a washing up bowl of radiator fluid in the garage. I came back and found her drinking the stuff. I don't know how long she'd been there, but she'd definitely drunk some. I can't say exactly how much."

The first thing to do was to make the Staffie sick. This is an easy thing to do, but a horrible job. Usually, veterinary surgeons are trying to stop cats and dogs from being sick! An injection of apomorphine works reliably. I talked Lottie's owner through the process so he knew what to expect.

Right on cue, ninety seconds after the injection, Lottie's cheerful expression changed. That unmistakable worried look appeared on her face and she started to wretch violently. Over the next few minutes, four piles of vomit appeared, just as I had predicted. I hoped a good proportion of the antifreeze would be included in what had come up.

The next thing to do was to provide an antidote to the ethylene glycol to counteract its catastrophic effects on the kidneys. The specific antidote to ethylene glycol is pure alcohol. Ideally this should be administered via a drip, but Lottie was very anxious and would barely stand still to be examined. I knew it would be almost impossible to place an intravenous catheter, let alone keep her sufficiently settled to allow the alcohol to run in slowly overnight. I also knew very well from experience that alcohol gets absorbed quickly and effectively when taken by mouth. I carefully worked out the dose. Plan B was to spoon measured aliquots of vodka into Lottie's mouth, every hour for the next four hours.

The next stop for Lottie and her owner was the off licence; they would just make it before it closed.

I checked her on Friday morning.

"How was the evening?" I asked.

"A bit strange," came the reply. "She fell off the sofa twice and I think she had a massive hangover this morning."

But Lottie showed no signs of kidney failure. The blood tests confirmed this. And so did her wagging tail.

The Great Yorkshire Show

5th July

This week has been remarkably quiet. It will have been the same in veterinary practices across Yorkshire, because this is the week before the Great Yorkshire Show. All our farmers – or at least the ones with show cattle, pedigree sheep and top-notch show jumpers – have had their minds and hands on other matters, in the final push to get their stock into perfect and pristine condition. Of course, the emergency stuff carries on in the same way as it does during any other week of the year, but routine jobs, like blood testing, fertility visits or trimming cows' feet are put off until a certain event in Harrogate has passed.

The run-up to the show is fraught with anxieties over the health and well-being of the potential winners. John called me to his farm to check on the progress of one of his Jacobs sheep. A couple of months ago, the gimmer lamb had been affected by a condition called cerebrocortical necrosis, which had caused it to go blind. However, John had caught it early and the young sheep had responded well to treatment. John wanted the final all-clear that she was fit for the ring, so that he could make his final selection.

It was a toss-up between two or three, he told me. Jacobs sheep have four horns and one would instinctively think that, to earn the coveted red rosette, the shape and symmetry of the horns would be of critical importance. I was surprised to hear that this was not so crucial. Body size, shape and condition and the shape of the white blaze running down the front of the face were most important. The sheep all looked fit and well. This, I could judge, but which would have the best chance of winning, I could not tell.

As farmers start to wash and spruce up their animals, we get a flurry of last-minute panic phone calls, to check on small blemishes – skin lesions that might be the early stages of ringworm or an abscess on the rump of a potential prize-winning heifer;

should we lance it and drain it, or would it be better to leave it to dissipate of its own accord and will it subside in time?

Early last week, Andy asked to me to visit his heifer. She had recently won first prize in a local show, but a small collection of warts had appeared on her teats. I called to see him and his lovely Aberdeen Angus heifer and assumed my customary position at the back end of a bovine, before lifting her tail. Sure enough, several warts, the size of seedless grapes, adorned the teats of the otherwise pristine animal.

"What can we do?" asked Andy. "I know they'll drop off eventually, but I don't want them to lead to mastitis and, if I'm honest, I don't want them spoiling her chances at Harrogate."

It is a simple procedure to remove warts from the udder of a heifer or the preduce of a bull and one we do frequently. They do regress of their own accord, but it takes many months and in the mean time they only lead to problems, as they get knocked or rubbed and become sore and infected.

"I think they'll come off a treat, Andy," I reassured him. "I'll need to numb them with local and put some rubber rings on."

This was easier said than done – injecting local anaesthetic into a sensitive teat, dangling right between the back legs of a lively young bovine was something of a challenge.

Fifteen minutes later, however, sweat dripping off the end of my nose, I had managed to encircle the unsightly growths with orange rubber rings, of the type used to castrate lambs and calves. It had been fiddly work and the immature udder looked like something from a balloon trick at a kid's party, but I was hopeful that the warts would quickly shrivel up and fall off. We both hoped that it would be in time. I'll find out on Tuesday.

GYS and RTS

12th July

This has not been the typical week of a veterinary surgeon in North Yorkshire.

On Friday night, I abandoned my wellies and waterproofs in favour of a dinner suit and black tie, to attend the Royal Television Society Awards in Leeds. *The Yorkshire Vet* had been nominated for an award in the "Documentary Series" category. Peter, the senior partner at Skeldale, who also features on the programme, was taking his turn on call back at the practice and, whilst I was sweating over what I might say if called upon to make an acceptance speech, he was sweating just as much, as – in the middle of a wind swept moor much – he struggled to replace the prolapsed uterus of a newly calved cow.

Possibly at the very moment that Peter managed to shove the very heavy, yet extremely fragile, uterus back inside the cow, a doyen of the TV industry in the North, dressed in smart white tuxedo and with glass of champagne in hand, took me by the arm.

"I just have to say, I love your programme," he enthused. "The best thing is, I just love the way you and your father work so well together. It's absolutely marvellous. My wife and I absolutely love Tuesday nights."

I tried to protest. I was certain that Peter would be less than thrilled to be mistaken for my father, but it was hard to interrupt without seeming rude, so I gave up.

"It's so great seeing father and son working together in such a lovely, traditional way. Like I say, I absolutely love your programme." And with that he was off.

Returning briefly to the veterinary world on Monday morning, my first job was to supervise and inspect the mating competence of several alpacas (again, far from a usual job, even for me). Back at the surgery, my sister was waiting, having driven up from Leeds with her cat, Daisy, who needed a check-up. Poor Daisy had been suffering from a nasty skin condition, which was stubbornly evading diagnosis. Every test I have done has come back with a confusing result so that, for now at least, I am simply treating the signs and scratching my head. It is typical that the pet of a close family member is such a complicated case! Thankfully for Daisy and our inter-sibling relationship, Daisy's sore feet were looking much better.

Then it was back to the world of competition for prizes. After collecting the kids from school, I loaded up our new camper van and set off for the Great Yorkshire Show, where I hoped I could lend some support to those farm clients and friends of the practice who were exhibiting their fantastic stock.

There were prizes for some, and disappointments for others. Five Second Prize rosettes for one farmer were a justifiable cause for celebration that lasted into the small hours, with large barrels of beer. Some had red rosettes and one friend won Reserve Champion with an enormous and very handsome Aberdeen Angus bull. For me though, the highlight of the show was meeting Geoffrey Boycott, my childhood hero, whom I bumped into at an amazing barbecue at the Welcome to Yorkshire stand.

"Oh hello!" he said. "I've seen you on telly. [Geoffrey Boycott had seen *me* on telly!] Me and my wife really love your show. We watch it every Tuesday night."

I really hope he didn't notice that my mouth had fallen open, and that I was rendered temporarily speechless.

The last word though, must go to the runners-up. I had been keeping everything crossed for my mate Martin and his Dairy Shorthorn. He was desperate to emulate the success of his forebears at the show, and bring home First Prize. Sadly though, and after so much toil and work and effort, this wasn't his year. It wasn't ours either – the Royal Television Society Award sits on somebody else's mantelpiece.

But runner-up, against stiff opposition is not so bad, after all, so both at the RTS and in Harrogate, we all celebrated!

Flynn from West Yorkshire

19th July

Every time I see Rodney, he presents me with a challenge.

When he saw me on TV, on *The Yorkshire Vet*, Rodney thought I would be a good person to look after his various animals. However, he was from West Yorkshire – his farm was just too far away from the practice. We need to be able to get to all our farms promptly in case of emergency. But Rodney was insistent that I should take charge of his sheep and goats.

"I can easy bring 'em up to see you," he implored. "I hardly ever have emergencies, you know, so I wouldn't be a nuisance." It was hard to argue. Cautiously, I agreed to take care of his small sheep farm and assorted collies. It was the beginning of a great working relationship.

The first time Rodney visited the surgery, he brought a car-boot full of little goat kids to have their horns removed. They chewed the equipment, weed on the floor and tumbled over one another as they capered around the prep-room. The job was simple but the mischievous kids caused havoc.

The next time it was sheep with a severe prolapse of the rectum. This serious problem quickly became worse as it subsequently ruptured, spilling out its small intestines; a prolapse within a prolapse. Most farmers, realising the seriousness of the situation, would immediately have thrown in the towel, but not Rodney. "If you think you can save her, do what you can…"

An hour later, and by some small miracle and much good fortune, "Lamby" was mended and heading back to West Yorkshire in the car boot.

His beloved collie, Millie, had a nasty tumour on her jaw, painfully invading the bone, distorting her face and teeth and making it difficult for her to eat. I managed to remove the front part of her

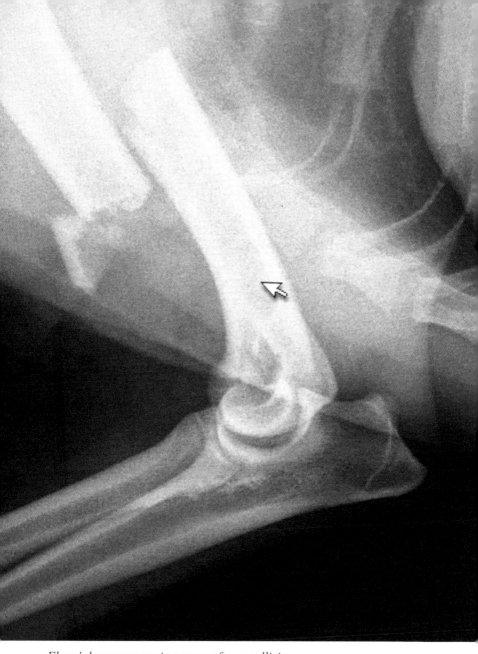

Flynn's humerus was in a mess after a collision when he was running around the farm.

jaw, in a procedure called a "rostral hemi-mandibulectomy". She continues to do well, some two years after her life-saving operation. She's just as lovely, and just as devoted to Rodney. I saw her a few weeks ago and she continues to thrive, years after the time when many owners and vets might have called time.

So, when my phone pinged last weekend, with a message from the on-call vet, to say Rodney had another job for me, I knew it would be something to test my veterinary skills.

Flynn, a collie who was related to Millie, was a two-year-old whirling dervish of energy. He'd been hurtling around the farmyard in the dark, and must have crashed into a tractor or some other machinery, because his right leg was badly damaged. There was a lot of bruising and he could not bear weight on it. My colleague had taken some X-rays, which showed a nasty fracture in the middle of the humerus – the main bone of the front leg that connects the shoulder to the elbow. Rodney was insistent that *I* should be the one to repair it, so when Monday morning came, all other jobs were rearranged. I rummaged around in the drawer of orthopaedic equipment to retrieve everything that I would need, going through, in my head, how I would approach the procedure. A fracture of this type lent itself to repair by using a bone plate, screwed onto the humerus to realign the fragments and restore the strength and stability of the bone.

The operation went well, and with the plate well aligned and sufficient screws to hold everything together, I was very happy with the result. Later that day, Rodney and Flynn were just as delighted to be reunited. As I waved them off, back down the A1 towards West Yorkshire, I knew that Flynn would be spending the next few weeks convalescing on the sofa in the house, instead of in his usual home in the barn with the other dogs.

I am looking forward to monitoring Flynn's progress over the next few weeks. I wonder what challenges Rodney's animals will present me with next.

Suki Relapses

26th July

Suki's treatment had been going smoothly. I had come to know her and her family very well over the weeks and months. I had monitored the variations in her blood cells, the dimensions of her lymph nodes and the subtle changes to her dietary preferences during the course of each chemo cycle. She would be a normal, happy dog for most of the time, with just a blip around five days after the three-weekly injection, when she would feel unwell. The only irksome issue was the right pre-scapular lymph node. It stubbornly refused to shrink and, whilst it did not seem to be bothering Suki, it was definitely bothering me. It was a sign that the cancer cells had not completely regressed.

Nevertheless, Suki was blissfully unaware of her illness. There is often some chit-chat in the waiting room, typically:

"What's he in for?" or "That's a big bandage – what's been happening to you?"

It is often the case that the seriousness of a chemo patient's illness goes unnoticed amongst the bandaged legs, limps, lumps or stitches of other dogs and cats. From outward appearance, Suki masqueraded as a normal dog.

As the weeks had passed, however, I was becoming increasingly worried about the size of her abdomen. Suki was getting bigger. It was ironic that, surrounded by the myriad of modern diagnostic techniques, like flow cytometry and immunohistochemistry, I reached for the tape measure, that we use to monitor fat dogs, to check on Suki's progress.

She was also paler than I would have liked and when I looked at the results of her most recent blood test, it became clear that, as Suki's girth was increasing, her blood cells were falling. It was time to put the tape measure to one side and turn to more sophisticated diagnostics. Suki needed X-rays, and I needed to take aspirates from both her spleen and her bone marrow, to establish whether the cancer cells had spread to other parts of her body. Since Suki was quite used to injections, the anaesthetic presented no traumas and she was soon asleep. The X-rays showed that the increasing size of her abdomen was due to a grossly enlarged spleen, which I carefully sampled. The bone marrow aspirate was slightly more fiddly, but my microscope slides and little pink sample pots were soon ready to send to the laboratory for detailed analysis.

Three days later the lab report arrived. It confirmed what I had feared. Lymphoma cells had invaded Suki's spleen and also her bone marrow. This explained why she was so pale and so round. A long and detailed conversation followed with Suki's owners, exploring all the possibilities. In the end, we decided to go ahead with a "rescue" therapy. This involved a complete revamp of the chemotherapy regime. Excitingly for me, the new drug, which needed to be run slowly and carefully into the vein in her front leg through a drip line, was fluorescent orange! As I hooked Suki up to the brightly coloured infusion, heads turned in the prep room – the usual fluid running through a drip is colourless.

Then came the best bit. Because the drug is quite toxic, it is important to supervise the animal closely while the infusion is in progress. It would be a disaster if the line were chewed or pulled out. This is what I tell the nurses when they walk past and see me sitting on a fluffy dog bed, cuddling my patient. It is the perfect excuse to sit on the floor and spend twenty minutes with my friend.

A week later, Suki came back in to see me. Her gums were pink and her abdomen was back to normal size. I didn't need my tape measure to see that she was plunged firmly back into remission.

There's a Foal Loose in the Lane

2nd August

"There is a foal loose in the lane," said the message in the daybook. It sounded more like a line from a Mister Man book than an actual veterinary visit. After a brief telephone conversation, I was on my way up the A19. I followed a little-used lane to the farm where the foal had been found.

I hadn't been to the farm before. The clients, Richard and Sophie, were new to the area and when I arrived they described, with amazement, the events that had unfolded the previous evening.

"We were just sitting outside, having a glass of wine and enjoying the evening sun," recounted Sophie, "when, all of a sudden, we spotted this little foal. It was just walking along the lane."

"We looked at each other," went on Richard, "and looked at our glasses and at the empty bottle on the table, and back at the foal. We couldn't believe our eyes. We expected a mare to appear, with a person to supervise, but there was nothing else. Just this little foal walking along the road all on its own."

Luckily for the foal, the lane was a very quiet one and there had been no traffic.

"He was quite easy to catch," said Sophie, "which was lucky, because we don't know very much about horses and even less about foals. We put a rope around his neck and lead him into one of these stables over here."

I was shown to a tumbledown stable, which, by the looks of its roof, its partly collapsing walls and the dry mouldy bedding, hadn't been home to an animal of any type for many years.

"Excuse the mess. We've not been living here long and we haven't got round to tidying up the outbuildings yet," she explained.

Lo and behold, there was a little colt foal, just a few weeks old,

"There's a foal loose in the lane," sounded like a made up line from a Mr Man book. This one was very real, though!

staring contentedly around, oblivious to its plight.

"We can only think it has been abandoned on the busy road," said Sophie. "We've checked all the fields and farms nearby and nobody has a mare that has lost its foal."

It seemed absurd that anyone would deliberately abandon a baby foal, especially so close to a busy dual carriageway, but people can do strange things and there didn't seem to be any other explanation.

I examined the foal in detail, and was surprised how friendly he was and how easy to handle. He stood calmly and confidently without a hint of anxiety or worry, as I prodded and poked him, listened to his chest, shone lights in his eyes and stuck a thermometer up his bum. He was a lovely little fellow!

The thermometer gave a high reading. The watery diarrhoea that appeared from the same end suggested that this was caused by an enteric infection. I started him on a course of antibiotics. Foals, or any young animal for that matter, with a bad start in life and away from their mother, are prone to picking up all kinds of infections and diarrhoea can be very serious, especially if there is a shortage of fluid to take in. It was critical that this youngster learnt quickly, how to drink from a bucket or a teat.

As a veterinary student, I spent some time at the studs in Newmarket, where I learnt that getting a newborn foal to accept anything other than its real mother was almost impossible. However, it turned out that a stubborn foal from North Yorkshire was a lot more resourceful than a delicate thoroughbred from Suffolk. He stuck his head straight into the ice bucket (from the previous evening's wine) which was now empty of ice but half full of artificial mare's milk, supplied by a neighbour. He guzzled it down with vigour. As frothy milk dribbled down the bottom part of his blaze and around his whiskery lips, we all knew that he would be fine. In many ways, this was a very, very lucky foal.

Two Youngsters with Opposite Problems

9th August

This week, much of my time has been devoted to dealing with the problems of two little black creatures, each residing at opposite ends of the hospital part of our kennels.

One of these creatures was a ten-week-old black kitten, who was very cute and very constipated. The other was a little black Labrador puppy called Lexi. She was also ten weeks old and also very cute but suffering from the opposite problem – chronic diarrhoea.

Lexi had been in with us for a few days. She was unconcerned by her condition, and jumped about and played with anyone who went to see her, but the diarrhoea was persistent, and she was on a drip and various medications, whilst we awaited results from the lab ("lab" as in "laboratory", not as in "Labrador" that is. The joke about "lab" tests wears thin after just a few weeks of being a vet. The joke about "cat" scans remains funny for a bit longer).

The kitten, who didn't have a name other than "Kitten", did not need any cat scans, though. The nature of her problem was clear by the roundness of her abdomen and fact that the litter tray had been empty for several days. Her worried owners had brought her in for treatment. Palpation of her abdomen identified rock-like faeces impacted in her large intestines. This is a common problem for young kittens and it needs to be rectified promptly. If the bowel wall gets very distended, it can be damaged beyond repair and lead to lifelong problems. The large intestine's role is to absorb water from the faeces, so if the wall becomes stretched and unable to contract properly, transit time is too slow and too much water is absorbed, making the faeces increasingly solid and compounding the problem.

The solution was to give the little kitten an anaesthetic so we could administer an enema of warm, soapy water through a rubber tube. The plan was gently to break down the concrete-like mass of faeces and remove the blockage. The addition of various lubricants can also help and every vet has a favourite combination of laxatives for this purpose. The task of unblocking a constipated cat is one that invariably goes to the youngest, most recently qualified vet. In this case, that person was Matt, who set about the job with fortitude.

Whilst it is a messy, smelly and painstaking process, it is also very satisfying, and a crowd of interested onlookers often develops. This was indeed the case this week, and a collection of vets and nurses all gathered to offer their favourite tips for removing the faeces.

After more than half an hour of inserting fluid into the back end of the little kitten, at least some of the impaction was coming away, and what was left in the colon was considerably softer. After the anaesthetic had worn off, "Kitten" clambered into her litter tray and, with legs akimbo and through half closed eyes, set about sorting out her problem once and for all. At the opposite end of the kennels, there was cause for celebration for the entirely opposite reason. At last, after nearly a week, Lexi had produced something solid! Ironically, her fluids had been going in through a tube at the opposite end of her body – the vein in her left front leg – to improve her hydration status.

Both little, black and very cute youngsters were heading in the right direction at last and would soon be heading home – one becoming softer and the other one firming up. It's a funny old job, being a vet.

Anal Glands, Vasectomies and 100th Hundred

16th August

It has been another week of contrasts.

I spent most of Wednesday morning stooped, peering at the perfectly shaved and scrubbed backside of Mitsy the spaniel. Mitsy was under general anaesthetic and blissfully unaware of this indignity, as I fastidiously and painstakingly dissected out her diseased anal glands.

Anal glands are an annoying inconvenience to most dogs, a remnant from their wild past. Nowadays, a dog's territory is demarcated by the garden wall and there is no role for these smelly glands. They can range from a minor inconvenience, to a painful problem if they become impacted, infected or even abscessated. In severely affected cases, the only option is to remove the glands surgically.

Mitsy had been suffering, on and off, for some time despite all our efforts to control the ongoing infection and inflammation in her glands. After an hour or so of careful surgery, the abnormal glands were sitting on my surgical drape, the op sites were neatly sutured and I could finally stretch my back and breath some fresher air.

Thursday afternoon saw me in a similar position, although this time there was no shortage of fresh air. I was on a sheep farm towards Helmsley, and my patients were a couple of very lucky young rams. They were lucky because they had been overlooked at the time of castration and so, at my suggestion, instead of being sent to market to be sold for meat, they were about to be vasectomised. These two would soon become "teaser tups".

A teaser tup is put in with a group of ewes two weeks or so before the real tups are introduced to the flock. The presence of active (though now infertile) males helps to bring the ewes into oestrus more quickly and all at a similar time, which results in a more

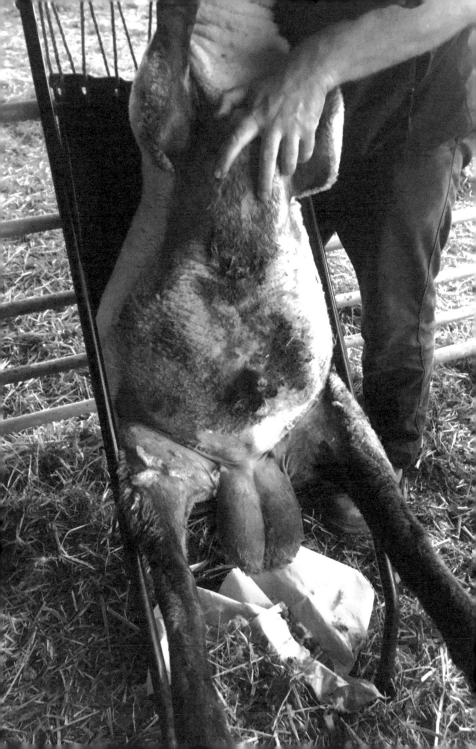

compact lambing schedule. Lambing can often extend over as long as six weeks, during which time the farmers become more and more exhausted as a result of working through every night. Adding vasectomised teaser tups can nearly half this time.

It was a win-win situation! It saved the two males from the butchers and gave them a lovely life, mating with ewes to their hearts' content, without a care in the world. Both rams behaved impeccably and, although the operation was every bit as fiddly as my previous day's surgery, I was soon stretching out my aching back again, cleaning off and heading home to have a shower and change into a suit.

My next appointment was in Boston Spa, as the guest of none other than Geoffrey Boycott and his lovely wife Rachael.

I had been invited to help celebrate the fortieth anniversary of Geoffrey's 100th First Class hundred, which he fittingly achieved in a test match at Headingley and, also fittingly, against Australia. The celebration was to raise money for The Yorkshire Air Ambulance – a brilliant cause and one, ironically, that almost made me late to the event, as one of the helicopters was in action, parked on the A1 very near to Boston Spa, attending to a serious car accident.

As my wife Anne was away with the boys, visiting her mother in Hampshire, my "plus-one" for the evening was my Dad. Scrubbed and in our best suits, we perused the seating plan. Imagine our surprise when it became evident that we were actually sitting on the same table as the great batsman and his family! I couldn't help but smile to myself in some disbelief, as I realised how completely this contrasted with the rest of my week.

Should this *really* happen to a vet?

Opposite: Vasectomising a tup is a very useful way to improve the breeding efficiency of a flock of sheep. The lambing period can be kept more concentrated.

Thirsk is Looking Lovely at this Time of Year

23rd August

The list of jobs stacking up on my pager looked rather like my final veterinary examination paper, as it seemed to involve pretty much every aspect of veterinary medicine and surgery.

A weekend on call starts on Friday morning and runs through until Monday, including the nights. Even before I had made it to the midway point of this particular weekend, I had accumulated an interesting array of cases.

A Wolfhound with severe pneumonia, a cat who had walked across a patio covered in weed killer, a Rainbow Boa (snake) with a bizarre swelling, a Labrador with hepatitis and an out-of-season-lambing kept me busy on Friday night and through into the early hours of Saturday morning. The lambing was the toughest of all, because the lamb was deformed and it took some manipulation to deliver it successfully.

Before morning surgery had even started on Saturday, the X-ray machine was in action. Griff the terrier had eaten a set of dental braces. The x-rays showed that Griff had chewed them up sufficiently to allow their safe passage without any further intervention. Next there was a hedgehog with a deformed leg to see, and later a bearded dragon with a prolapsed rectum. I could only look longingly at the tray of mugs of coffee that had appeared, as I headed out to see a pony with laminitis on the far side of town.

I drove through the middle of Thirsk, which was busy and bustling, with locals doing their shopping and visitors soaking up the sunshine and the sights. The lovely market town that I have the privilege to call home was looking particularly beautiful, adorned as it was with flowers and the colourful woolly accoutrements that have been attached to every bollard and post by the "Thirsk Yarn Bombers". These covert knitters were first inspired to "yarn bomb"

The "Yarn Bombers" have spent many hours decorating Thirsk with woolly decorations. They started to coincide with the Tour de Yorkshire which came through the town in 2016.

Thirsk when the Tour de Yorkshire came through in 2016. The inhabitants of the town woke up one morning, a couple of days before the cyclists arrived, to find knitting adorning trees, lamp posts, bus shelters and shop doorways. It has become quite an attraction, and visitors come from afar to be photographed with the woolly things. But perhaps the most peculiar woolly creations of all are the life sized, knitted Julian and Peter in a shop window, along with a knitted cow, recreating a scene from *The Yorkshire Vet* television programme. It is quite startling to drive past a shop and see yourself immortalised in knitting!

The number of visitors to Thirsk seems to be swelling. A recent survey showed Thirsk to be number six in the list of top places to visit in the UK. In the last two days I have met people visiting from Northern Ireland, Scotland, Leicestershire and Devon, because they have seen our welcoming town and our beautiful countryside on *The Yorkshire Vet*. Everyone benefits – the coffee shops, the museums, the bookshops, the fantastic old Ritz Cinema. It is amazing.

But I didn't have time to enjoy an ice-cream or fish and chips with the tourists in the market square. I had a lame pony to see and its owner was worried. My beeper was making its presence felt again. A dog was shaking and vomiting, a guinea pig was lying down and not moving, and another horse was suffering from colic. I still had plenty to do and there was a lot of my weekend still to go.

In a Field in the Middle of Nowhere

Morning surgery was just about at its end as I injected Alfie, a cheerful cocker spaniel, to reverse his sedation. I had been investigating a large and painful swelling above his right upper canine tooth. There was pus coming from the gap between the tooth and the gum. The X-rays did not show anything sinister, so I was hopeful that the swelling was simply a tooth root abscess.

Alfie was an elderly dog with a multitude of problems, but he stubbornly continued to defy the odds and his little tail would always wag. I added yet another tablet into his daily concoction, to control the infection, then went to phone his owner to relay the news. As I made the phone call, my eyes scanned the daybook to see what my next job would be.

"Cow in field. Not right. Visit please – phone first for directions"

This seemed a bit strange, as I visited the farm regularly, but having finished speaking to Alfie's owner, I called the farmer as requested.

"Ah, I'm glad it's you Julian. You're just the vet I need for this cow. She's lugubrious, you see. More to the point she's in a field in the furthest away, most inaccessible part of the farm there is. It needs a man with a good vehicle, otherwise you'll never get to her."

This sounded like an adventure.

"Go past the farmhouse, turn left along the track into the woods and after about quarter of a mile turn left. The track gets bumpy and narrow. Just before it turns into a path, turn left through a gate. You'll know it's the right one 'cos that's where the mud starts. Through that gate and down the hill and she's in the field at the bottom. You'll see the tractor. If you get stuck give us a ring." And with that, he was gone. I wondered whether he meant stuck as in lost, or stuck as in stuck.

I put Alfie's tablets in a bag and left strict instructions for the nurse to pass on to his owner, including apologies for not being there to see her myself. Then, I collected all the medicines I might need to fix a "lugubrious" cow.

As I set off, I considered the case ahead. There were two problems facing me. Firstly, the description of the cow as lugubrious meant that its signs of illness must be very vague. A coughing calf, a lame cow or a lambing sheep are easy to treat, but a vaguely ill animal is much more difficult – in the words of James Herriot "if *only* they could talk". Secondly, it seemed likely that actually getting to the patient at all would present a greater challenge than usual. I could picture the first part of the journey, but I had never ventured beyond the woods. The description of mud and steep hillsides suggested I would be gone for some time.

Sure enough, when I found the gate where the mud started, it was clear my off-road driving skills were going to be put to the test. John, the farmer, was on the far side of the gate, half way down the hill, which was of Sutton Bank proportions. He was waving me towards the best route to follow, so as not to take off my exhaust pipe on the uneven, rutted hillside. My trusty Mitsubishi has never let me down, and, if I'm honest, I loved it!

Eventually, I got to the cow. The diagnosis was much more straightforward than the journey. She was suffering from tracheitis. I injected two big syringes of medication into her jugular vein.

Now, how to get back…?

My trusty Mitsubishi gets me to the most challenging places. This morning's job was more difficult than most, but there was no need for help from the farmer's tractor!

Katie the Cat, Stuck on Flypaper

6th August

Edwin was waiting in the car park when I arrived at work on Thursday morning. The small plastic box on his passenger seat looked odd in such a large van and he quickly jumped out, clutching the box, when he spotted me driving in.

He usually came in to the surgery with a border collie.

"I didn't know you had cats, Edwin. Is everything OK?" I asked.

"It's my little cat, Katie," he replied. "By heck, she's all bloomin' well clarted up with sticky fly paper. By, she is gummed up."

He went on,

"Daft thing is, this stuff is blummin' rubbish at sticking flies, but it hasn't half stuck *her* up good and proper."

The retired farmer followed me into the surgery with his sticky cat.

It took some time to extricate Katie from her box. "I think she's stuck!" said Edwin, without a hint of irony. When she finally emerged, it was immediately obvious that it wasn't just gluey flypaper that was causing a messy problem for Katie.

"I tried to clean her with Swarfega," Edwin explained. The combination of glue and goo on feline fur was not a happy one.

The only thing to do was to sedate the cat and clip off all the affected bits of fur.

De-matting (or in this case, "de-gluing") a cat is a very satisfying job but one usually reserved for veterinary nurses. In this case, however, there was no way I was going to miss out. I knew it would be every bit as rewarding as all the other jobs written on the board, waiting to be done:

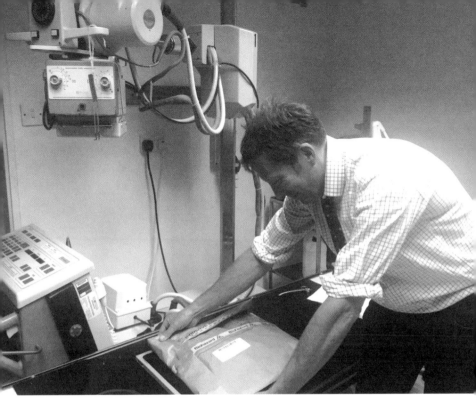

*X-raying a padded envelope was not what
I expected to be doing today and I was sure
the bird was deceased. It was an ex-bird.*

GA X-ray R stifle +/- surgery

GA bitch spay

GA X-ray hips and lumbar spine

3x GA cat castrate

GA pluck ears and clip nails - CARE

Sedate to de-glue cat

Half an hour later, Katie was sorted. One half of her body was smooth and hairless and the other was pretty normal. A bath and a brush later, she was as good as new, although looking rather peculiar so I hoped she was not due to enter any beauty contests in the near future.

I telephoned Edwin to reassure him that Katie was un-gummed and absolutely fine, and could be collected at lunchtime.

I moved on to one of the next things on the list. Patsy, the elderly terrier, had badly damaged her right stifle and it did, as suggested, require surgery. The procedure went very well and she, too, was soon awake and comfortable in her kennel.

At the end of the morning, an extra, not so happy procedure was added to the ops list. It arrived in a large, padded brown envelope.

"Can you X-ray this, Julian?" asked the head nurse. "The police have dropped it off. It's a peregrine falcon. They think it has been shot."

As if the arrival of a dead falcon, in a large padded brown envelope was not strange enough, the label, which was stuck to the outside, was enough to tip us all over the edge into hysteria. There was a long strip of yellow tape, which proclaimed "biohazard" and a label with a string of reference numbers and a bar code, followed by a description of the contents of the envelope. It read:

"Deceased (believed) juvenile peregrine falcon"

I felt as if I should first reach for my stethoscope to confirm the deceased nature of the bird, since the description only said *believed* (to mis-quote Monty Python – it was, in fact, definitely deceased. It was an ex-peregrine falcon).

Strange as it was to be X-raying an envelope containing a dead bird, the most surprising thing about our morning's exploits was that only half of the assembled nursing staff, vets and ever-present camera crew were aware of the existence of the amazing substance called "Swarfega".

Deadly Nightshade or Deadly Lampshade?

13th September

Evening surgery had finished and another busy day was drawing to a close. Since I was on call, it fell to me to deal with the list of telephone messages that had accumulated during evening surgery. First, I spoke to a lady about her horse. I had seen it a week or so previously, with a swollen leg. It had completely resolved with the medication I had prescribed, but had filled up again after the medication had finished – could she have some more?

Next, I reported the blood results of a beagle who was losing weight and drinking excessively, and then I had a long discussion with the owner of Rufus – a sheltie with more problems than you could imagine – about a lump that was becoming a worry; did we really need to operate or would a custom-made sling (to hoist the dangling lump) suffice to save the geriatric dog from another appointment with my scalpel?

The final message was to call Mrs Lawson about her dog, Bert, who had eaten some Deadly Nightshade. This sounded serious, mainly because the plant had the word "deadly" in its name. The dangerous compound in Deadly Nightshade is atropine – a drug with important medicinal uses. It is used regularly in veterinary medicine in the form of drops, to dilate the pupils of a dog or cat with uveitis (an inflammatory condition of the eye) and, in its injectable form, it is always part of a "crash kit" for emergencies: it can be used to increase a dangerously low heart rate, particularly during anaesthesia. Dilated pupils were once seen as very attractive, hence the plant's other name – "Belladonna". Unfortunately, in a non-diseased eye, a dilated pupil allows too much light to flood onto the retina. This causes great distress, which is not so attractive.

So back to Bert.

"He loves eating berries – especially blackberries," explained Mrs Lawson. "We were out walking and I stopped to chat to a friend. I looked down, and Bert was licking his lips and making a face. When I went to investigate, I could see some berries and I'm certain they are from the Solanaceae family. He is absolutely fine, but for me, this is history repeating itself."

She went on to describe how, several decades earlier, her daughter had done the very same thing. The little girl was rushed to hospital to have her stomach pumped. Some weeks later Mrs Lawson's son confessed to having eaten just as many poisonous berries as his sister. Having seen the horrible stomach-pumping episode, he had decided to take a chance with the berries. Luckily, he was fine.

As we weighed up the pros and cons of inducing vomiting versus the likelihood of poisoning by the "deadly" plant, the tension was broken by Becky, one of the camera team, who was ever alert to a good story.

"What's this I hear about the dog?" she exclaimed. "The one that has eaten some deadly lampshades!"

Having assured a slightly embarrassed Becky that lampshades were not toxic to dogs, I arranged to call and see Bert on my way home, to make sure all was well.

As I rang the doorbell Bert came rushing to greet me, barking and wagging his tail. He looked absolutely fine. I shone my pen-torch into his eyes. His pupils were only slightly larger than they should have been and both constricted nicely under the light. The three of us all agreed that no emergency stomach emptying was needed and, rather like her son had done years before, Bert got away scot-free.

Bantam with a Bandage

20th September

"And now I've got a bantam for you to look at," shouted Michael. Michael was very deaf, which meant that consultations were usually carried out at high volume.

I had known Michael for many years and, as his hearing had slowly deteriorated, I found that writing my questions and subsequent diagnosis on a pad of paper made life much easier for both of us. I had spent the last few minutes scribbling down notes about his border collie. The dog was suffering from chronic diarrhoea and, Michael had shouted, it was imperative that the problem should be fixed "before the nights get too cold." Apparently, the door to the conservatory was left open during summer to allow the collie emergency access outside during the night. This wouldn't work as the warm nights of mid-summer slipped towards autumn. Michael wanted to remedy the problem, as much to make his dog better as to keep the house warm.

Having sorted the collie, I turned my attention to the bantam. She had been caught in some mesh a couple of weeks previously and received some treatment, but was still not quite right.

Michael lifted the little bird out of her box and set her on the table. He pointed to the left leg and bellowed, "It felt a bit hot."

The left foot looked swollen and as I examined it, smelly liquid oozed out of a small hole near one of the claws. I reached for my note pad and pen. Trying to write legibly, I explained that the skin over the foot had become necrotic and needed to be removed. Michael nodded in agreement.

"I have another bantam who has a problem with her wing," he shouted. "She has now become something of a pet bantam and lives in the house. I have a feeling this little bird will follow suit!"

I set about trimming off the dead and devitalised tissue – it came away very easily and without the need for an anaesthetic, since there was no sensation. Underneath, there was a bed of healthy, but delicate, granulation tissue. It needed to be protected with a bandage. I applied some "blue spray" – the cure-all for anything like this (it used to be purple until regulations forbade the use of the gentian violet that made it so) and injected some medication into her other leg. Then I reached for my pad and pen, *"watch what I do, because you'll need to reapply a bandage like this every two or three days,"* I scrawled. I bandaged the foot and handed extra bandage materials to Michael, before bidding bantam, collie and owner goodbye.

My next patient also had a sore digit, but this patient was not a bird. Nor was it a dog, cat, cow or sheep. This sore digit belonged to a well-known radio presenter, with whom I had just enjoyed a cup of coffee whilst discussing the arrangements for the forthcoming "Yorkshire Vet at The Countryside Live" event at The Yorkshire Show ground. As I was about to leave (to see a recumbent llama) the well-known radio presenter asked, so politely that I could not refuse, "Julian, can you just have a look at my thumb. There is a swelling near the end. Look!"

I prodded the swelling and was about to ask if it hurt, but the immediate yell told me the answer. I should have asked if it hurt before I started the prodding.

Two minutes later though, in the carpark of the coffee shop and with the help of a hypodermic needle from my well-stocked car boot, the abscess had been lanced. It was a very similar problem to the one experienced by the bantam, although without the need for blue spray, or a bandage.

"Oh Julian, you are marvellous!" enthused the well-known radio presenter, as pus seeped from the end of her thumb. "Thank you *so* much. It's stopped hurting already."

Another happy patient, I thought as I rushed off to see the llama.

The bantam was looking happier after I'd cleaned its foot.

Lame Llama

27th September

I called in briefly at the practice to collect Laura and her camera. The farm where the llamas were kept was at least half an hour's drive away, over in Nidderdale. As we got closer, Laura switched on her camera, pointed it straight at me (as usual) and began quizzing me about the visit; what I might expect to find when I got there, what might be the nature of the problem and how serious it might be? I didn't really have any answers for her. All I knew was that the llama was flat out in the field and couldn't stand up. It sounded very serious, and I suspected that the outcome might be a sad one.

We arrived at the farm and, as I gathered everything I thought I might need to treat a collapsed llama, I scanned the nearby pastures for my patient. All the animals I could see were grazing happily.

It wasn't long before Suzanne, to whom the llamas belonged, appeared. Since the panicked phone call to the practice, she explained, the llama in question, whose name was Aztec, had been coerced to his feet and coaxed into one of the buildings. He was already in the specially made crush-cum-stocks arrangement that keeps these long-legged animals standing and restrained in just the right way.

"We managed to get him up just after I'd called," said Suzanne, "but he doesn't look happy. His ears are back and he's not eating properly. He's an old boy, but it's just not like him, so I'm glad you're here because I'd like him to have a proper check over."

I started, as usual, at the head and worked my way back, examining each part of the body and asking questions as I went. Was he lame? Was he wobbly after he got up?

The only clue came from Suzanne's comment about his gait.

"He was walking with his back legs apart, as if he was sore around

I love treating llamas and have enjoyed learning about their various problems over the years. Nidderdale is an unusual place to find these creatures, but they have made it their home!

his back end."

This made sense. Any kind of pain around the back legs could have caused him to have difficulty when he tried to stand.

My examination had taken me to the appropriate part of his body and I lifted his tail to take his temperature. It was at this point that the cause of his problem became clear. Poor old Aztec's bottom was ulcerated and very sore. It had been sore for some weeks –

Suzanne reminded me that I had briefly looked at it earlier on in the summer, in passing, when I was on the farm treating other animals. She had been regularly applying a salve-like ointment, which had provided some relief, but this was much worse than I remembered.

The lesion looked quite sinister, and as I probed with my lubricated finger, it became evident that the thickened and painful area extended several centimetres inside his rectum. I was concerned that it could be a cancerous growth. We discussed all the options. It was impossible to make any further clinical decisions without a diagnosis, and so I embarked upon a procedure I had never done before: an anal biopsy on a llama. It was more straightforward than we all imagined it might be. I administered an epidural so that the whole area was completely numb, and this enabled me to take two biopsies of the abnormal tissue. I put the two little samples in a formalin pot, ready to send to the lab. The results will be back next week. We all have our fingers crossed...

Aztec's Bum

4th October

There was an anxious wait both in Thirsk and in Nidderdale for the results of Aztec's biopsy. I think both Suzanne and I feared the worst. I had administered some medication after the sample was taken, simply to ease some of the discomfort and reduce the inflammation. Reports came back from Nidderdale that Aztec seemed to be back to good health; his ears were up and his appetite was back to normal. He'd even completed two treks over the weekend. Were it not for the peculiar lesion around his bum, nobody would know anything was the matter. My initial treatment had proved palliative, but the analysis of the biopsy would hold the key to his future. I peered at the fax machine every time I was in the office, willing an answer to appear.

In the middle of the week I was presented with another interesting patient: a bateleur eagle with a bad eye. It was at The Birds of Prey Centre, Sion Hill, just outside Thirsk. Colin, the falconer, had told me about this bird. It had a persistently runny right eye, and he had taken it to see a falcon expert, but nothing had been found and the bird was no better.

"Could you come and have a look?" he asked.

I am not an expert on falcons, but an eye is an eye, with just a few subtle differences between birds and mammals. I'm interested in eyes and ophthalmology. I reasoned that the causes of a watering eye in a bird would be broadly the same as in any other patient that I had treated so, armed with an ophthalmoscope, I set off to see what I could do.

The bateleur eagle – a handsome black eagle with an enormous red beak – was out of display and ready for my examination when I arrived. Sure enough, its right eye was watering profusely, causing the feathers underneath to matt together. I watched it fly, seemingly unaffected by its problem. It was magnificent to watch. Kerry, the handler, even let me have a go with it on my arm. I was an avid ornithologist as a kid and I could have stayed and done this all day, but I could not put off the inevitable close-up examination any longer. The sore eye was perilously close to the massive red beak and I was anxious about what might happen to my nose if I peered too closely. Fortunately, the examination, in a perfectly darkened shed, was much more straightforward than I had imagined. Even better, I managed to identify the reason for the watery discharge. There was a collection of ingrowing feathers on the lower lid, rubbing on the surface of the eye and causing irritation. I had seen this many times with extraneous hairs in fluffy Cavalier King Charles Spaniels or Shih-tzu puppies, but never in an eagle. But, as veterinary surgeons, we learn to adapt and work from the principles painstakingly instilled into us during our years at vet school. The treatment was the same whether the cause was a feather in the eye of an eagle or an excess of hair in a puppy: the offending bits needed to be removed.

I instilled some anaesthetic drops into the eye and reached for my forceps. Kerry held the bird with expertise and within moments, the three offending feathers had been plucked from within the lower eyelid. Various jokes were made about the patient soon being "eagle-eyed" again, none of which were very funny.

When I got back to the surgery, Aztec's lab results were waiting. The news was not good. Despite his obvious improvement after the treatment I'd given him last week, his results were what I expected but not what I hoped. The llama had a tumour.

There was some hope, though. This particular type of tumour can be treated with a drug called bleomycin. It is injected directly into the lesion, so that it is active only very locally and thus, the side effects that can come with chemotherapy are mitigated. The tumours often regress to manageable proportions, either so that they can be removed surgically, or so that they cease to cause too much of a problem. I used this treatment for the same type of tumour, but in a cat's tongue some years ago, with good success. Suzanne was keen, as long as it didn't involve any unnecessary discomfort and it would afford some relief.

But bleomycin is a human drug and hard to come by. Neither our normal veterinary suppliers nor the local pharmacist were able to obtain any. I called the pharmacy departments of numerous hospitals across the north of England, but they could not help either. All I could do was to keep Aztec as comfortable as possible while I continued my search.

This bateleur eagle, belonging to The Birds of Prey Centre at Sion Hill, had a peculiar and ingrowing feather in its eye, which I managed to remove under local anaesthetic. I saw him recently and he's doing very well.

Camper Van at Kielder

11th October

Last week was a busy week. With two nights on call, miscellaneous interviews to promote the new TV series and three book signings to squeeze in around work, the weekend seemed to be a long time in coming. However, as I finished my last visit on Friday lunchtime, it was finally time to head out on our first family camper van adventure.

We had been thinking about getting a van for years, but a few months ago, we decided to stop pondering and actually do something about it.

Anne followed up an advert for a van for sale in Tewksbury. It looked exactly what we were after. It turned out that the previous owner had bought the van to take his daughter, who was a good swimmer, to swimming galas all over the country. This was an amazing coincidence, as it was also one of the reasons now was the time for a van for us. Our youngest son, Archie, swims in galas all over the North East of England, while Jack, our oldest, rows on rivers up and down the country. Staying in the van would mean less driving and more time in bed before a 7.30am start on poolside, or a 6.30 start on the river.

Two more amazing coincidences quickly followed. It emerged that the swimmer was also a budding veterinary student and spent her Saturday mornings at the local veterinary practice – the very same veterinary practice, in the Cotswolds, where Anne and I had both worked, before we came up to Yorkshire. Clearly, this was destined to be our van, and the deal was quickly done.

So, this weekend, we headed north, to Kielder in Northumberland for Anne to run in the Kielder half marathon, following the forest tracks around half of Kielder Water. Its big brother, the marathon, circumnavigated the entire lake. Jack and Archie were also racing in the junior race. For a change, I was just the support crew, along with Emmy, our dog.

Northumberland was so quiet and so free from traffic that it made the roads around North Yorkshire look quite hectic. 4G was soon left behind, quickly followed by the 3 version and soon we had no phone reception at all. It was nice to be able to abandon mobile phones and lose the distracting "ping" of another Whatsapp message.

It was a clear and still evening and, as the sun set over our campsite, we awaited the much-anticipated "Draconid" meteor shower. This part of Northumberland is proud of its status of having one of the darkest skies in the UK, so we were expecting a spectacular display. However, not long after darkness fell, all four of us were fast asleep, utterly oblivious to the shooting stars overhead.

Race day dawned all too quickly but, for once, it wasn't me feeling the nerves. Normally, the phrase "race day" has me brimming with excitement that has been building for weeks. This morning though, I took charge of the coffee and bacon sandwiches, as we packed up camp and headed for the race.

Anne was off first, setting a good pace. Jack, Archie, Emmy and I skimmed stones across the still waters of the lake, whilst we watched the full marathoners go past the start line. The junior race was next. Archie led the Norton brothers up the first hill, but positions had changed by the last 400 metres. Jack finished an impressive eighth in a competitive under sixteen race. Archie, on the other hand, limped in, nursing a swollen knee and, Jonny Brownlee-style, spent more time in the first aid tent than he had on the course.

Sore knees apart, it was a great weekend and lovely family time, without phones, without vetting and for me, without a race. I could get used to this. Maybe I'm getting old?

Cow in the Mud, Cleansing and a Book Signing

18th October

My first call on Saturday morning was not a happy one. I was half way through my breakfast when the phone rang. I'm never good in a morning if I don't get to finish my coffee, but this was an emergency. An elderly Highland cow, more of a pet than a production animal, who we had been treating for severe arthritis for some time, had fallen and become stuck in a muddy ditch during the night. The farmer had found her when he went on his morning rounds to check the stock. He thought the time had come to say goodbye to this old girl. I arrived and stumped across the fields to find her. It was terribly sad but at least the end was quick and painless for her.

Back at the practice, morning surgery came with its usual selection of new puppies and booster vaccinations, punctuated by a variety of ailments and injuries. Mixed veterinary practice has an amazing knack of tempering a run of sad cases with a serendipitously placed happy outcome. Princess, the tortoiseshell cat was just such a case. I had spent much of the previous evening trying to sew her back together. She had been out on cat adventures and returned as usual, at teatime. One of the children had spotted a sore patch near her tail. When I examined her, I found a huge laceration, which had ripped out all the skin under her tail and across the back of her legs. She was in a proper pickle. Despite the obviously serious nature of her injury – the cause of which was unknown – she continued to purr throughout my examination. It took two hours, and more sutures than I could count to reconstruct the mangled tissue but, as I checked her on Saturday morning, I was amazed at how good the surgical wounds looked. Better still, she could pass urine, so there had been no serious damage to her urogenital system. We just needed to wait and see if the lower part of her bowel still worked. I was happy to see her progress as she tucked into a bowl of her favourite cat treats.

The next job was a cow with a retained afterbirth. It was a long ride to the farm, up Boltby Bank, but the countryside was beautiful as the leaves have started to hint at their autumn colours. I had to keep my eyes firmly on the road though, as a multitude of cyclists were out enjoying the autumn sun.

Treating a retained afterbirth in a cow is simple but smelly. The placenta fails to come away after the calf has been born and dangles down from the back of the cow. It quite quickly starts to decompose and can lead to infection developing inside the cow's uterus. The main challenge is to stop the fetid smell of decomposing placenta seeping into the skin of one's arm. One plastic arm length glove is not sufficient. I have come to know that no fewer than four layers of plastic are necessary to allow a lunchtime sandwich to be eaten without concern.

My last visit was altogether easier. It was nearby and it was not smelly. I had an appointment with Ken and June in their lovely bookshop, Claridge's of Helmsley, where I had arranged to meet people and sign copies of my new book, *A Yorkshire Vet Through the Seasons*. As I pulled up, only slightly late, with my pen in hand, I had no intention of letting anyone know exactly where my right arm had been, just thirty minutes before!

I Think She Needs a Caesar

25th October

I was negotiating my way out of the carpark, heading out to see a horse with a sore leg, when one of the receptionists came rushing out, clutching a piece of paper.

"Change of plan," she called. "There's a Caesar to do. Can you divert and go there instead? The horse can wait, it didn't sound urgent. Jack, on the other hand, is worried about his cow and wants a vet as soon as possible."

"Excellent! Of course," I called back, stopping the car. "Tell him I'm on my way." I love the excitement of an urgent calving. It is a thrill that has not subsided over the twenty-odd years of work in mixed practice. It was also good news for Laura, my near-constant companion over the last two and a half years, her camera ever at the ready. A calving was much more appealing to the camera crew than a boring old horse with a sore leg (horses, for some reason, are not nearly as good for the TV as cows and sheep).

As I pulled into the spotless concrete yard, I saw Jack, the farmer, who greeted me with enthusiasm.

"She's in here, come through," he beckoned. "It's a big one and she missed a calf last year so she's got too fat. It'll need a Caesar, I'm sure. Have a feel if you want, but I've got everything ready for you."

I was ushered into the calving pen, where a beautiful conker-coloured Limousin cow was standing politely behind a gate on an immaculate straw bed. Two feet were pointing out of the cow's

Opposite: A happy mother and a healthy calf mean a happy farmer, especially after a natural delivery.

back end, upside down, indicating an obvious problem. Either the whole calf was upside down with its head back, or the calf was coming out backwards. The latter was the most likely situation and the easiest to deal with. Fortunately it did indeed turn out to be the case. The calf was quite large and it was tight in the pelvis, but the feet were not enormous. I thought it was worth trying for a normal delivery, despite Jack's assertion that it would need a scalpel and a side route out.

It was a tense few moments for everyone. I felt the calf would come, with just some gentle traction from my calving machine but Jack was not so sure. This is always a precarious situation. We have all made the incorrect decision at this stage at some point in our careers. One too many pulls on the calving-jack and the calf is stuck or the cow is injured, or both. Despite the experienced farmer erring towards surgery, I was erring towards a natural birth, and, with reservations, Jack conceded that it would be worth a try.

The cow was oblivious to our quiet negotiations. I let her do the pushing and simply applied pressure to "take the strain" between each wave of contraction. Before long, the calf's pelvis popped into the mother's pelvis and the worst was over. Half a dozen more pulls and the bull calf slid to the ground and nearly landed on top of farmer and vet. Calves that come out backwards do not have the benefit of the mucus and fluid being squeezed out of their lungs as they are delivered, so we hoisted the new-born over a gate, allowing mucus to drain from his nostrils, clearing his airways. As usual, it worked a treat and he was soon sitting up in the straw, looking for a teat.

Jack and I enjoyed a few moments of mutual congratulation as we watched the mother and calf form their all-important bond.

"I read your column in the *Yorkshire Post* every week and I love it!" grinned Jack. "I wonder whether I'll feature in it next week?"

As I snapped a quick picture of cow and calf, I think he already knew the answer.

Let the Cat Out of the Bag

1ˢᵗ November

Patients arrive at the surgery in an array of containers. Cat boxes and baskets are the norm, and most veterinary surgeons dealing with pets have a detailed knowledge of the wide range of cat receptacles available – and, crucially, how they open and close (which can be surprisingly complicated). My personal favourite is the cat container with semi-rigid sides that can be completely unzipped. With just a few deft manoeuvres, the three-dimensional bag can be rendered completely flat, leaving the cat simply sitting, slightly confused, on the examination table. It is a brilliantly simple design that removes the need to grapple a frightened cat from the back of a plastic box.

Some cats come to the vet in "hold-all" sports bags (although fewer now than in years past). The surprised face of a cat, as its head pops out from the small gap in the zip, always makes me smile. I can never resist the obvious "shall we let the cat out of the bag?" joke. It's still hilariously funny even after twenty-one years.

A shoebox or plastic tub with holes in the top usually suggests a different type of pet. It will be small, it might be furry or feathery, and it will definitely bite. Some vets have even been known to make an excessively long and thorough examination of their previous patient, in the hope that a colleague will have called in the small, furry, biting creature in the shoebox before they re-emerge from their consulting room. Obviously, this is not something I have ever done.

Two ferrets came in recently, in a rucksack. The side pockets were filled with ferret accessories – snacks, water bottles, coconut paste and salmon oil (ferrets love these and it facilitates an easy examination), harnesses and hammocks.

The strangest receptacle of all though, I encountered last week.

Tricia was standing patiently in the waiting room. She had no cat basket, no dog on a lead, no rucksac, no bag and not even a shoebox or plastic tub. I presumed she had come in to seek advice about one of her horses or another member of her menagerie.

I called her into the consulting room, where she started to tell the story of a baby chick, which she had seen hatch out of an egg the day before.

"He just popped out of the egg and stood there, Julian, on the dirty path," she explained. "His mum was nowhere to be seen, so I kept my distance and watched him for about half an hour. But no mother appeared, so I thought I should rescue him. I didn't think he'd have any chance by himself. Anyway, I've brought him in for a check over."

I still couldn't see a little bird anywhere.

"Here he is! He's been living in my bra to keep warm," announced Tricia, as she undid the top buttons of her blouse to reveal the fluffy face of a little yellow baby chick. I wasn't sure what to do next. Luckily, Tricia scooped him out and put him on the table.

It is not very easy to examine a bird this small and all I could really do was offer advice. He looked healthy enough, despite his rather unconventional start in life. What Tricia also wanted to know was the sex of the little chick – we were calling it "he" but, really, it needed to be a girl if it was to join the rest of her flock. But she was to be disappointed, as I explained that to sex a day-old chicken was impossible for normal people. It is a highly skilled (and highly paid) job that only a handful of people in the country know how to do.

As the little chick was nestled back in its most comfy of carrying cases, we both hoped it would thrive. From an unpromising start in life on a dirty path, his chances had considerably improved now he had found a cosy new home.

Cats come to the vets in all manner of containers, usually a basket or cage, but today's patient was in a bag!

Jess and the Bum Bandage

8th November

Jess was just two years old, but already I knew her very well. She was not an ill dog – far from it! The effervescent, young springer spaniel was the picture of health, but she was very accident-prone. Beneath her cute and innocent exterior was a dog who acted first and thought later. Except that more often than not, she didn't bother with the thinking part.

Her clinical notes catalogued a series of over-exuberance related injuries and ailments. Thankfully, they were mostly relatively minor. There was conjunctivitis brought on by diving into some bushes, a sore nose as a result of sticking it repeatedly down a hole, a bout of diarrhoea triggered by swallowing a whole rotten rabbit carcass and a case of laryngitis caused by eating a pile of grass on an early morning walk. She was a regular visitor.

Even the relatively simple process of a routine spay along with removal of her extraneous hind dew claws had caused more difficulties than was usual. Jess was determined to remove every bandage that was applied, which resulted in multiple re-dressings and a re-stitch.

This time, Jess's problem was her tail. As you can imagine, Jess's tail was rarely still. Its constant and furious wagging, as she barged her way through hedges and ditches in search of adventure, had resulted in some nasty scratches where brambles had become tangled in her feathery fur. Jess had then set about licking and chewing the sore places, as only she knew how, and in no time at all, the end of her tail was one big oozing wound, which was both painful and messy. The white parts of her fur were stained a rather delicate shade of strawberry pink.

As I peered at the angry lesions, it was clear there was only one course of action that would solve the problem.

*Poor Jess looked much happier after the
bandage on her tail did not obstruct her bum!*

"I think we are going to have to amputate it, I'm afraid," I explained. There was no need to dance around the subject. Tail injuries, especially in dogs like Jess, are extremely difficult to deal with using the simple means by which most wounds can be treated. Constant wagging, knocking and chewing results in a sore that never heals. Removing the diseased end is often the only course of action to take. Jess's owner, Mrs Smith agreed. She was relieved that there was a solution.

By the end of the week, the op had been done and Jess was back in action at home, her slightly shorter tail neatly bandaged. Everything went smoothly for the next few days and Mrs Smith even became skilled in replacing the dressing herself, saving frequent trips back to the surgery. However, when I saw Jess for her next check-up, Mrs Smith told an unusual tale.

"Well, Julian. I thought I'd got quite good at re-bandaging the tail – the first one I tried fell off, but the second was OK and the third, well, I thought 'this is a beauty – it's never going to come off'. I'd put extra tape on and it was great. Anyway, later that evening, as I took her out for a final walk I noticed that she was straining a bit. I thought to myself, 'Oh no! Not a bout of colitis, that's the last thing we need, what with a tail bandage and everything'. She came back into the house and then I thought, 'What's that strange smell?' and then I realised – I'd bandaged the tail but also her BUM! I was mortified! She was trying to go to the toilet but couldn't because my bandage had gone all the way round her bottom! I felt awful and I cut it off immediately. I hope there's no lasting damage!"

I removed the bandage, carefully and examined the tail end – it was healing well. I also inspected the bottom. Thankfully for all concerned, the bottom was fine.

The Greedy Sheep

15th November

"Julian, could you have a word with this lady about her sheep, please?" asked Sandra, our new-but-already-very-competent receptionist. It was a familiar request, but it turned out that the topic for discussion was not one that I had encountered before.

"The sheep have broken into the tack room," explained the anxious client, whose name was Joan. "They have climbed onto the rug box and eaten all the rat poison!"

This sounded more like a scene from a *Wallace and Gromit* cartoon than a real-life mishap in Cold Kirby. I had visions of the Swaledales standing on each other's shoulders in some kind of ovine pyramid, so that they could reach the poisonous feast on the top shelf.

It is quite common for a greedy dog with an indiscriminate appetite to succumb to this type of poisoning but I had never seen it in a ruminant. Goats do have a penchant for munching on all sorts of rubbish, and hungry cows for gorging themselves on cow cake, but sheep eating rat poison was, for me, definitely a first.

I started to ask some questions, while wracking my brains for an appropriate course of action. Was she *sure* it was the sheep who were to blame?

"I know it was the sheep," Joan confirmed, "because they are all sheltering under the roof just outside the tack room and there is sheep poo and open packets of poison everywhere. The problem is, I don't know which sheep have done the eating. It might be just one greedy one or it could have been all fifteen."

The camera crew from *The Yorkshire Vet* gathered, somewhat like vultures, ever alert to an interesting story, as I continued my conversation on the phone.

"Do any look ill?" I asked hopefully.

"No!" came the exasperated reply. "They all look absolutely fine. To be honest, they actually look quite pleased with themselves. Turquoise granules are spread all over the floor so I'm sure they have eaten some. I suppose I can't say exactly how much for certain. Oh dear, what a nuisance. Naughty sheep!"

That the sheep looked absolutely fine was exactly as I had suspected. The toxic effects of rat poison manifest as a failure of the blood clotting process. Illness usually develops a few days after the poison has been eaten, as a result of internal haemorrhage. It was very unlikely that any would be showing illness at this early stage. So, the question remained: what to do?

If a dog has eaten rat poison, we instigate vomiting to empty the stomach; we can test for clotting deficiency, and we usually start treatment immediately. The antidote to rat bait is Vitamin K, which we inject in the first instance, and then follow up with daily tablets – for up to *three weeks*, which is the length of time that the poison can persist in the body.

This was clearly not going to be a practical solution for fifteen sheep, but it seemed reckless not to do anything. We couldn't make them sick, blood testing each of them to look for an increase in clotting time was unlikely to be reliable, and administering Vitamin K every day for three weeks to the whole flock would be eye wateringly expensive, as well as very difficult. I suspected that the smallholder's budget would not run to such a course of action.

Then a plan came to mind:

"We should try to establish exactly which of the sheep, if any, have eaten the poison," I told Joan. "It's turquoise – so if you keep them in individual pens overnight and check their droppings in the morning, we should be able to identify the miscreants."

It wasn't ideal, but we both felt it was the most pragmatic solution to a very odd problem.

As I put the phone down, I think we both felt that at least we had a way forwards. The only people who were disappointed were the camera crew, who drifted off, to other parts of the practice to look for another story…

Jack Russells

22nd November

"Are you quite vocal then?" said Sharon, the receptionist, to my next patient, as he burst into the waiting room with his owner. It was a rhetorical question, and, quite quickly, superfluous. Alfie, the diminutive white and black Jack Russell Terrier had started as he meant to go on. He spent the next ten minutes making his presence felt to everyone in the waiting room, both human and animal. He barked and pulled on his lead, trying to make acquaintances with all the other pets, as he waited his turn on my morning list of appointments. A busy waiting room is a great place for a sociable terrier to hang out – the canine equivalent of a youth club, and the ageing terrier had lost none of his youthful vigour when it came to meeting and greeting. He barked almost constantly, to the point where the other humans were beginning to roll their eyes.

Finally, after what may have seemed like an eternity for the other patients and their owners, Alfie's name was at the top of the list. As soon as he came into the consulting room, I could tell that he was a typical Jack Russell. He knew what he liked and he knew what he didn't like. Luckily for me, he quite liked vets. I soon discovered that he didn't like his temperature being taken.

Mr North, Alfie's owner, got straight to the point. "I brought him to see you, Julian, because I know you are a 'Jack Russell Man'."

I took this as a compliment, although some people may not have done so. Mr North was quite right – I do love these tough little dogs. I was brought up with them. Our current Jack Russell, Emmy, is every bit as brilliant as the wiry terriers of my youth. She is long-in-the-body and short-in-the-leg and (very) rough coated. What she lacks in stature, she more than makes up for in enthusiasm for life. I suppose that is what makes the two of us so well suited. She, too, knows what she likes (swimming, running,

My Jack Russell, Emmy when she was a pup. She was cute then and is just as endearing now! She's a very devoted dog and she happens to be very photogenic. A good addition to any vet photo shoot!

playing ball, staying at "Auntie Julie's" and playing with her best friend "Titch") and what she doesn't like (squirrels, fireworks, spotty dogs and rain). Like every Jack Russell, she is unswervingly loyal and would follow me to the end of the earth. Like so many other Russells, who go along with their owner in a tractor or a van, Emmy loves to jump into the car with me, and watch out of the window, as I head off on my calls.

This morning's Jack Russell, Alfie, had a nasty cough, which was made worse by the excitement of getting up in the morning and pulling on the lead. I have never met a Jack Russell that doesn't pull on the lead. As I examined Alfie, carefully at first – just in case he changed his mind and decided he didn't like vets after all – it became evident that he had a very sore windpipe, exacerbated by all that pulling on his lead. He had a nasty infection called "tracheitis" which would need some medication. Luckily, this fairly common problem is quite simple to treat. Relieved, Mr North went on (as Jack Russell owners often do) to describe the special relationship that had developed between him and his dog, from the very beginning, when Alfie was a little pup, right up to the dog's slightly belligerent dotage.

Without a glimmer of a smile to suggest he was joking, he said. "He's a decent dog. He gives us some grief, but, on balance, he's worth having."

Not a ringing endorsement, but I knew exactly what he meant!

Last Weekend on Call – Pharyngeal Stick

29th November

My latest weekend on call was typically busy and varied. A caesarean on a heifer started the action on Friday evening. The farmer knew what was needed, and when I arrived, the expectant mum was already fastened up with a halter, in a cattle crush modified especially for the procedure. During the very first caesarean section on this farm, the farmer had hastily cut a hole in the side of a gate to allow surgical access to the left flank of the patient. This homemade arrangement was perfect and we now use it every time. He even had two buckets of warm water ready for me!

Having finished morning surgery on Saturday, I went to visit a horse – Ed the thoroughbred – with a swollen leg. I sensed trouble when I arrived at the yard to see the owner, Catherine, arguing with Ed about whether to come in from the field.

"Can you fetch another lead rope?" she shouted to me, before I had even got out of my car. Her plan B was to bring two horses in together, in the hope that this would calm the anxious patient. However, I thought it would be easier to examine Ed in the field, despite the mud. Ed's cellulitis was caused by a nasty, infected crack above his heel bulb – painful and sore but fairly easy to fix.

My most challenging case of the weekend came next. Barney, a six-year-old Labrador, was very poorly. His owners were both concerned and confused in equal measure. They could not understand how he could have gone downhill so quickly. However, from the telephone conversation I had with them, I had a fairly good idea what the problem might be. He lived on the edge of a wood and his favourite hobby was chasing sticks, thrown by his owner. When I met him and his owners at the practice, Barney was standing, reluctant to move, with his eyes half-closed and with a string of blood-tinged saliva hanging from the corner of his mouth.

"Oh yes, he loves his sticks, old Barney," confessed his owner. "I know I shouldn't throw them for him, but it's just not a walk if he hasn't got a stick."

Barney's temperature was sky high, suggesting that infection was already well established. I carefully opened his mouth and, although it was painful, the cause of his problem was clear. He had a large gash under his tongue surrounded by blood clots and gloopy debris. Closer questioning revealed that there had been an incident on his morning walk. He had let out a squeal as he tried to retrieve a stick, stuck into a grassy bank.

Barney needed urgent treatment. Stick injuries can often extend deeply into the tissues of the throat. It is important to explore – with an endoscope if necessary – the full extent of the damage under general anaesthetic, as small pieces of stick can cause life-threatening infection if left in the depths of a penetrating wound. Luckily for Barney this wasn't the case, but the laceration was about ten centimetres deep and I flushed it with antiseptic solution before suturing the gash back together. I once had a similar injury in my own mouth (having been kicked by a horse – but that's another story) and I know how painful it can be. Suturing the wound takes away much of the pain, stops it from filling with food and speeds recovery.

After the surgery, along with a bag of intravenous fluids and some antibiotics, Barney's temperature returned to normal. By morning, he was looking all together happier. The lucky Labrador trotted out of his kennel when his owner came to collect him, none-the-worse for his accident.

A firm resolution was made *never* to throw sticks for him again.

Opposite: An injury to the underside of the tongue is typical of a "stick injury". These can be very serious, especially if the penetration is deep down the throat. Barney was very lucky.

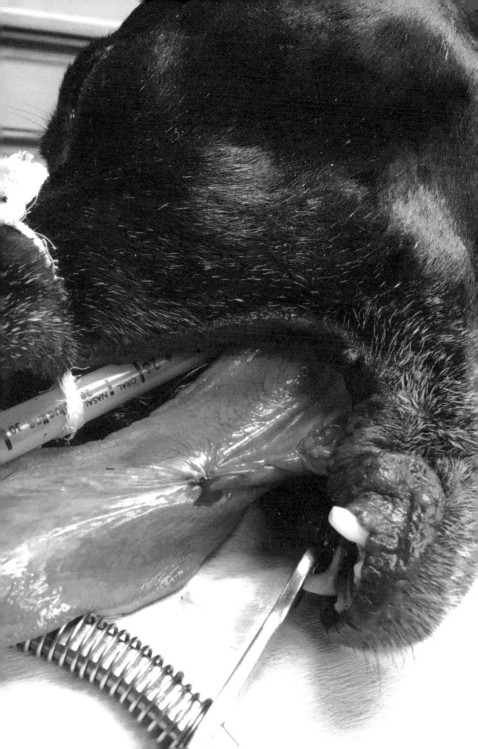

Pregnancy Testing on Snilesworth Moor

6th December

It is a stretch to consider travelling along the twisting and undulating road that leads to the middle of Snilesworth Moor as work. Yet this was exactly what it was as, on Monday morning, I left the flat of the Vale of York and headed for the rugged wilds of the Hambleton Hills. The rest of my day would most certainly be work – there were sixty or seventy wild suckler cows to pregnancy test and I knew it would be hard.

Pregnancy testing suckler cows, as they are housed at the onset of winter, is a perennial job for any large animal vet. It is crucial to check each cow, to make sure that she is pregnant. For hill cows like those I was going to see today, who eek out an existence on the rough food of the moors, life is tough. They do not go into winter with an excess of fat, like cattle grazed on lusher lowland pastures. For the farmer, it is equally tough, and if a cow is not pregnant, it is not economical to feed her during the long winter months. My job was to feel inside the rectum of each cow and palpate its uterus, hopefully to feel a tiny calf bobbing around inside. I love this sort of visit, although it is not one that every vet would rush to put their initials next to in the daybook.

As well as the perils of having to avoid the kicking feet of semi-wild, barely handled cattle, Monday was a wild day and the cold wind was laden with sleet. At least we were under the cover of the Dutch barn, albeit with its open sides.

The cows had been gathered off the moor just that morning, so it had been an early start for Mike and his two sons. For all it was cold, wet and windy outside, the cows, along with their strong, six-month-old calves, did not really want to be inside the farm buildings and they charged around, looking for means of escape back to the moor that was their home. Persuading them that it was a good idea to go into the cattle crush, which was at the end of a long race, was an even bigger challenge. Once a cow was standing still and safe in the crush, I could get in behind, to do my thing.

All eyes were on my facial expressions, as I rummaged around inside each cow. A quick pronouncement usually meant a positive diagnosis and everyone's mood lifted. If I vacillated, it usually meant that I could not feel a pregnancy. Any "empty" or "geld" cows would be heading to Thirsk fat market as soon as her current calf was weaned. It seems harsh, but this type of farming is a harsh life, and there is little room for sentimentality.

Everything was going well. The final stubborn few cows were corralled into the collecting area. The long, dirty and at times dangerous job seemed to be nearing its end.

"That's good," said Mike, happy with the result of my testing. "Forty-four out of forty-eight pregnant. Better than last year." I began to think of my warm car. "Now we just have the next batch to do. They're at the other farm, at the other side of the hill. We'd better crack on, 'cos they're not used to being handled either. That batch will take just as long as all these!"

As I set off, following Mike in his pickup to the next venue, I knew it would be some time before my hands regained any warmth and several more hours before I would be having my lunch.

"…With Broken Tools,"

13th December

Last week was not an easy one. Usually, this would mean an overdose of nights on call, a weekend on duty with disrupted sleep, long TB tests on wild cow herds in cold places, or a challenging surgery extending well beyond what could have been a lunch break. In recent years, for me, this might also have meant the pressures of having a television crew following me, searching for an entertaining story.

But last week's challenge was nothing to do with clinical pressures, or those connected with the media. I was leaving the practice in which I had worked for over twenty years; a place where I had spent more time than any other, and one where I had experienced a catalogue of emotions with both my patients and their owners and the exceptional staff with whom I have had the enormous pleasure to work. Animals I had delivered, vaccinated, neutered, watched grow old and, patients whose lives I had saved (I'm thinking of you, Tess) or cats in their dotage who I had nurtured through a myriad of complex illnesses (I'm thinking of you, Sid).

In recent years, I have shared many of these experiences with the world, through the brilliance of the production team from Daisybeck Studios, based in Leeds, who created the television series *The Yorkshire Vet*. This has added an extra dimension to the richness of many cases, with the knowledge that it was not just the nurse, the dog, its owners and me who would be intimately involved.

So yes, it was a difficult week. Here is not the place to discuss the reasons, nor is it the time. I was moving on. It was the end of an era and that was how it had to be.

"Have some time off," suggested (if not implored) Anne, my wife. "A week or two, to relax, have a lie in and take it easy – at least up 'til Christmas."

She was, of course, completely right. I could definitely have done with a bit of a break, but this is not really in my nature, as well she knew. A day visiting primary schools to talk to some year six pupils about writing books, and a morning at the Herriot Hospice Homecare followed by a lunchtime talk for a Yorkshire Cancer charity was as much of a break as I had allowed myself.

The notice outside my new practice in Boroughbridge. I never expected that I'd be leaving the practice that I loved so much in Thirsk. But times change and I had to move on.

I had agreed to help out an old friend – a veterinary surgeon practising not too far from Thirsk. He had been short of both vets and time-off over recent months and I had offered to lend a hand. As I familiarised myself with the inner workings of his practice, I could imagine the golf clubs were already being swung.

Being in a different practice brought with it a whole new set of challenges. I headed out to pregnancy test a beef suckler herd, but had no clue where I was going. In Thirsk, I knew every farm and every country lane, and I could navigate from place to place without a thought. Now, I needed satnav, a map and several phone calls to confirm I was heading in the right direction. First farm found, I had to establish the best place to park my car. It sounds simple, but I knew the perfect parking place on every farm around Thirsk. Now I had to learn these from scratch again.

Cows tested, all was good and I headed back to the surgery. Evening consultations were starting and I didn't want to be late. The first appointment was a simple vaccination. What could possibly go wrong?

But it was not straightforward: the veterinary surgeon with years of experience couldn't find the syringes!

Christmas Dinner

20th December

Tuppy was a Norfolk terrier and he was on his holidays with his family. A trip to spend the festive season visiting friends in North Yorkshire had seemed like a great idea. Everyone was enjoying the frosty weather and the twinkling Christmas lights in our lovely market towns, and Tuppy had settled in nicely with the friends and their cat.

But the seasonal cheer was rudely interrupted when Tuppy grabbed the cat's toy in his mouth. His owner saw him do it, and tried to retrieve the toy, but Tuppy, typical terrier that he was, had different ideas. He refused to let go. In the ensuing skirmish, the toy was swallowed – whole. The cat was obviously upset, but it was Tuppy who was to come off worst.

After a day of vomiting, without the toy re-appearing, the inevitable phone call to the vets was made.

"It's our little terrier! We are on holiday, visiting our friends for Christmas and he's swallowed a small cat toy. Now he's being sick. Do we need to bring him in? I hope he doesn't need an operation."

The usual questions followed: "How many times has he been sick?", "Is he poorly?", "Does he have diarrhoea?" (vomiting is often part of a more general gastroenteritis condition and the toy swallowing incident might have been a coincidence) "When did it happen?" And then, crucially: "Was it a toy that belonged to a small cat or was it a toy in the shape of a small cat?"

Questions are critical to help a veterinary surgeon establish a suitable course of action.

"It's the toy that belongs to our friends' cat," confirmed the distraught owners. "It's a mouse. Not a real one, obviously, but it looks like a mouse and it's about the same size, except it has long

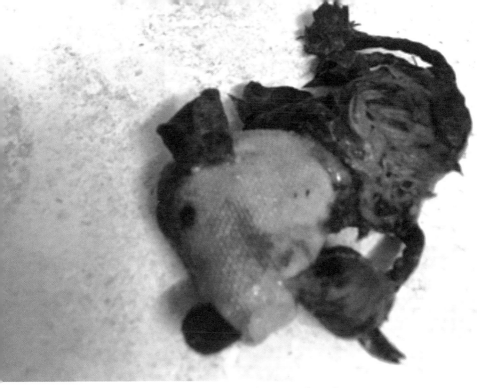

An unusual, and not very tasty,
Christmas dinner for Tuppy.

arms and legs. It's made of material and it has a long tail. Well, it
doesn't have a tail now because I think I pulled it off when I tried
to get it out of his mouth."

The final comment meant that I did not really need to ask the final
and most crucial question: "And did he *definitely* swallow it?"

The toy was of a sufficient size to be a big problem for a terrier
and it would be very likely to get stuck in the lower part of the
stomach. This was why Tuppy was vomiting. It was a classic
presentation, but not the classic Christmas related foreign body
we usually see at this time of year. More usually it is the contents

of a Christmas cracker, a length of tinsel or part of a turkey. Decorations from the Christmas tree also make a tasty festive treat for a non-discerning dog, confused about the purpose of a tree inside the house.

But un-festive as it was, the mouse needed to be removed from Tuppy's stomach, and we set about the necessary preparations for surgery. The assembled vets all had different ideas about the merits of exploratory surgery versus removal by endoscope, but eventually we decided that operating would be a quicker and more reliable way of extricating the mouse.

An hour later, Tuppy was sitting up, sleepy and a bit befuddled, but with a neat row of sutures down the middle of his tummy, and no mouse inside. He would soon be home to enjoy a restful time relaxing beside the fire. The mouse, meanwhile, was lying on the side in theatre, smelly and stained. It didn't look at all well, but after a soak and a cycle in the washing machine I knew that it would soon be back in action as the cat's favourite toy. I hadn't asked if it had been the cat's Christmas present.

Lost on the Way to a Lambing

30th December

I had not got lost on the way to an urgent farm visit for many years. Yet, at half past twelve last Thursday night, in the week between Christmas and New Year, that was exactly what I was – lost.

The call was a garbled one. A farmer had a sheep to lamb and needed a vet. He repeated this message several times, along with the farm name. Establishing exactly how to get to the farm was not so easy. I rarely need to rely on the satnav, preferring instead my trusty OS map, but I typed in the postcode late that evening and hoped for the best. I kept my map as plan B and set off into the darkness, relying, for the first time, on the computer in my car to find a sheep in distress.

I had a vague idea where to go, and after several loops of the nearby village, the pleasant but insistent voice coming from the dashboard of my Mitsubishi assured me that I had reached my destination, which was on the left. On the left was a children's playground. Through the darkness, I could make out the vague shape of some kind of rocking horse, but no heavily pregnant Suffolk. My map wasn't much more helpful. I needed a plan C. The telephone number was no good – it was a landline and I knew the farmer would be outside, readying buckets of warm water, bars of soap and towels for my arrival. I had a vague recollection that he said he would wait by the farm gate with a torch. Plan C involved driving around the dark lanes of Asenby, in a semi-random fashion, looking for a man holding a torch.

After about ten minutes, and more by luck than judgement, I had actually arrived at my destination, which was, indeed, on the left. There was no farmer with a torch to guide me in, but the name on the gate confirmed I was in the right place. It was a beautifully clear and frosty night and the lane up to the farm, beyond the gate, was lit up by a full moon. I wished I had the camera crew with me

– it would have made a lovely scene to set the beginning of a story on *The Yorkshire Vet.*

I could make out the stooped form of the elderly shepherd in the lights of the open-sided lambing shed as I donned my wellies and grabbed the things I would need.

I clambered over the makeshift pens. "Sorry I'm a bit late! I got lost." I could offer no better explanation.

"Not to worry," he replied. "She's over here; been on a while. I've had a feel and that lamb feels awfully big to me. And my hands, well they're not so good these days. I struggle with any that are tight. I must've had you vets out about ten times so far this lambing time." He showed me to the patient. There were several mothers – all pedigree Suffolks – already with fit, strong lambs. I hoped my efforts would yield another couple of healthy lambs.

As we positioned the mum-to-be in a suitable place and I scrubbed my right arm, we chatted about his lambing time so far and how it was going – big lambs, small lambs, plenty of twins, not too many triplets, how many he had left to go – "just about a dozen now – I'm nearly there."

I gently felt for the lamb. There was a head and front legs and, yes, both did feel very big. It would be tight, but with some gentle persuasion and plenty of lube, I was confident the lambs would be delivered without too much problem. Sure enough, two healthy twins were soon shaking their heads and flapping their ears in the straw. This evening on call, finding the farm had definitely been the hardest bit!

Acknowledgements

The Diary of a Yorkshire Vet is my third book. It is briefer than my others, but has been every bit as enjoyable to write. It is based on my *Yorkshire Post* articles and chronicles fifty-two weekly veterinary stories throughout 2017. As such, I have to give enormous thanks to Ben Barnett, editor of the *Yorkshire Post*'s "Country Week" who, firstly, persuaded me to commit to writing a weekly column and secondly agreed to using these stories as a basis for this book. Thank you, Ben, for both these things.

Thanks, too, to David Burrill from Great Northern Books, for agreeing to publish this book. It's brilliant to be able to work with local businesses and this is something about which I am passionate: local communities are so much better and so much richer when we all work together.

Thank you to all the clients who have featured (albeit usually under pseudonyms) in these stories, and also their animals, whether they are cows, pigs, sheep, horses, dogs, cats or ferrets. Without you and your fascinating animals, this book would not exist, so thank you for the inspiration! North Yorkshire provides a rich vein of stories, that's for sure!

I am particularly grateful to Alan McCormack and John Sommerville for giving me the opportunity to come and work at their practice after I left my job in Thirsk. It's a lovely place to work and provided me with the perfect antidote at exactly the right time. Not only have you provided me with the opportunity to continue my passion and love for mixed practice in North Yorkshire, it also allowed me the chance to continue writing about stories of mixed practice in our wonderful county.

My family and close friends have been, again and continually, utterly supportive of all my mad-cap work during the last few years, both on screen, behind the laptop and beside the cow. It's not been an easy year and without their help and support, I'm not sure that this book would exist. Thank you – you know, you kept me sane!

Anne, as ever, this book wouldn't be half as good without your input, adjustments, tweaks and comments. The combination seems to work as well in literary terms as it does in life! Here's to the next one?

The diary of a Yorkshire vet
5869869

Kirby
Wiske

Thi

Pateley Bridge

Harrogate

G